A GECKO IN THE MACHINE

Postcards from the Bahamas

AuthorHouse™
1663 Liberty Drive
Bloomington, IN 47403
www.authorhouse.com
Phone: 1-800-839-8640

Published by AuthorHouse   11/27/2012

ISBN: 978-1-4772-4637-5 (sc)
ISBN: 978-1-4772-4638-2 (e)

A GECKO IN THE MACHINE

Postcards from the Bahamas

Michael Heslop

authorHOUSE®

ACKNOWLEDGEMENTS

I would like to thank all those whose expertise generously given, have made this book possible:

Gillian Nicholls for having read the (very) early rough draft and commented so tactfully:

George Skipper for his photographic help:

Supportive friends (you know who you are!):

The people and winter residents of Exuma who have shown us a thing or two about how to enjoy life:

And last, but not least, my long-suffering wife without whose encouragement this would undoubtedly not have seen the light of day.

Any errors of fact, misunderstandings and all flights of fancy are entirely my own.

Michael Heslop
2012

To my family

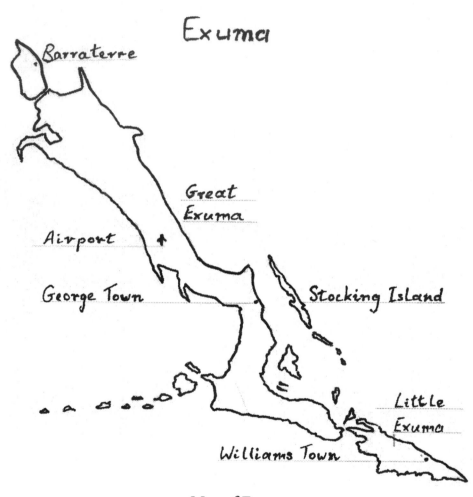

Map of Exuma

CHAPTER 1

"Do you know Exuma?" said the voice.

"Never heard of it," I replied.

"Come over in November for a week and I'll show you round."

We did and loved it: the beauty, the warmth, the people and the peace.

But this is how it all began . . . .

"Listen to this." I exclaimed in disbelief. "A piece of paradise for just £3500!"

Depressed by endless monochrome grey UK skies, (if you blink in the north of England you may very well miss the summer), we had spent five years looking for a better climate to live in, principally in the Mediterranean. But having slid off mountain roads on black ice in Turkey and been snowed on in Corsica, we concluded that the winters in the Med were just as bad as in the UK, if not worse. Sitting at home one winter's evening in front of a roaring log fire with a good glass of red wine, I put down the Sunday papers and picked up a copy of the National Farmers Union magazine "Countryside"; in the classifieds was that advertisement. I continued, "Look at this: its just absurd!"—A palm tree reclined lazily over a provocatively coral sand beach upon which lapped a somnolent turquoise sea. "How unreal can a photo be?" And dropped the offending magazine onto the floor. After some moments of silent contemplation I murmured, "That was a local telephone number you know—what have we got to lose?" and muttering to myself, retrieved it.

I was connected to a man called Peter Clements who has since become a good friend and who was a UK agent for a property company in the Bahamas.

The Bahamas is tax exile country but we certainly did not fall into that category. What compelled us was the pace and quality of life, year-round warmth and sunshine. One of the things that struck us most forcibly, however, was that so far as we could tell there was a complete absence of any racial prejudice, despite our being in a minority of about 5%. We were treated with courtesy and good humour. And plenty of the latter as the Bahamians have a naturally sunny, friendly temperament projected by foghorn laughter and megaphone vocal chords.

Exuma is a beautiful, sleepy member of the Bahamian "out-islands" lying in uniquely striking, pale, limpid turquoise waters and straddling the Tropic of Cancer. The colour of the waters arises from their shallow depths over pale coral sands and the fact that there are no rivers in the archipelago to pollute the sea with silt. In all, the Exumas are about 70 miles from tip to toe. About 41 miles long and 9 miles or so wide, Great Exuma tightens its waist at the "Ferry" bridge and becomes Little Exuma. To the North 365 small islands and reefs known as "cays" stretch over 40 miles up towards Nassau, the Bahamian capital on New Providence island, some 100 miles away. In the centre of these cays lies the impressive Exuman Land and Sea Park comprising 112,000 acres of serene and pristine natural beauty. Our search was ended.

Let the real work begin and three more years of searching for the right site, obtaining planning approval and builders, not to mention supervising the build from, mostly, the UK and we are ready to move home to the Caribbean.

CHAPTER 2

It is Monday 15th November and a new life begins today for my wife Linda, our German Shepherd dog Habu and me. After seven years of sifting, looking and, finally, building, we are emigrating to the new house we have built on Exuma in the Bahamas. Having spent months planning and executing increasingly small and fiddly "to do" lists we are off. The day starts early as a hire van is collected in Newcastle some forty miles from our home in Northumberland. This transport is essential to move our luggage and the dog's air travel kennel, a vast and palatial edifice of plastic with mesh "windows" and door supported upon four heavy slide-on detachable wheels. Instructions from various pet organizations including DEFRA seem to indicate that its internal space should be large enough to indulge in field sports.

The journey to Heathrow is uneventful taking about six hours including leaving our trusty Volvo with friends to store. Arriving at our destination, however, an eternally watchful Murphy's Law decides to throw us a first curve ball. We discover that there seem to be half a dozen Holiday Inns at Heathrow and roll up to most of them before we manage to find the one we have actually booked into: very few hotels at the airport will take dogs. This diversion takes us an additional two and a half hours and we are weary not to say mildly hysterical on our final arrival.

Next morning we are up well before a frosty dawn to walk the dog. Realising that I will never find our way to the terminal to drop off spouse and dog and then drop the van at the hire depot, we hire a taxi to lead us and then return me to the terminal after the drop. The driver is Indian and a star: without him we would have had a collective nervous breakdown but after sitting in airport rush hours and waiting at traffic lights whilst vast passenger aircraft trundle across the road (yes, really!) we finally alight with all paraphernalia at the correct terminal building.

Presenting ourselves at the check-in desk we have to wait for an experienced porter to come for the dog and kennel. Habu (a rescued police dog who failed his exams because he licked the villains instead of biting them) is a credit to his breed and training, sitting on his haunches and silently watching the insanity that is human ants and Heathrow on a busy morning. After more than an hour a lugubrious porter arrives and exhibits no "special pets knowledge" whatsoever. We put Habu in the kennel and the porter insists that we take him out again so that he can check the kennel for contraband. Given that the kennel consists of a single layer plastic mould and the dog's only comfort within is a small thermal rug it is difficult to understand where such illegalities might be stowed. The porter leaves to find a trolley and once again we are left to our own devices in the maelstrom. Departure time is now looming large and so we accost the desk asking what is happening. There seems to be no progress: nobody knows any thing about us and nobody cares.

"I can't do any more of this; I just want to go home," my wife wails at one point.

"You can't let our dream of a new life be destroyed just because of one recalcitrant porter; you know we're stronger than that!" I respond with concern.

Then new staff appear and after some mumbling amongst themselves the manager turns to us and announces, "We're a new shift team and I've some bad news for you—the plane is boarding now and we are going to have to leave you behind because you aren't checked in."

Apoplexy ensues.

"We've been standing here for two and a half hours," we yell, "waiting for you people to organise yourselves." Where is the porter who went to get a trolley an hour ago and has never come back? They relent: a trolley appears being hauled by a new porter (this despite the fact that the kennel has its own wheels which then cause considerable trouble as it keeps threatening to slide off the trolley) and we are frogmarched to the plane. As we climb the steps to the aircraft we look along the fuselage and see that the ramp to the luggage hold is still connected.

"Is our dog on board?" we ask.

"Not yet, but come in and find your seats," comes the reply. Our moment has come. "Then we aren't moving."

"Come along, he'll be here in a few moments."

"ABSOLUTELY NOT!—WE AREN"T MOVING ANYWHERE UNTIL WE SEE HIM LOADED."

"No, no it'll be all right."

"NO!" Then the kennel arrives and we see him moving up the ramp in stately fashion. We board to meet the stares of the other 300 odd homicidal passengers who regard us, balefully, as the sole reason for the delay of their flight. We find our seats and my wife dissolves into tears. Notably, the flight staff are horrified by our treatment and are very understanding which at least repairs some of the damage done by the ground staff. We are finally properly on our way, although a subsequent official complaint to the airline is met with complete indifference. Nevertheless, we have a life to get on with and little time to waste arguing with them.

The outward flight is uneventful and we arrive in hot, sunny Nassau, the capital of the Bahamas, without incident. A Bahamian immigration lady looks at our passports and, seeing the pages filled with Bahamas entry stamps, beams at us and says "welcome home!" We move over to the baggage conveyor belt to wait for our luggage and suddenly at the entrance a small and extremely vociferous whirlwind appears. It is Habu in his kennel/cage who has seen us and on release goes completely berserk with excitement. He leaps round and round, jumping and howling and barking all at the same time. The customs officials are highly alarmed and we are ordered to get him under control immediately. This takes some little time as we are scarcely under control ourselves; being reunited after the havoc of Heathrow represents a very moving moment for us all.

We grab a porter to collect our various cases; he loads up his wooden flatbed wheelbarrow-wheeled trolley and we sail through customs. "They got nothing to declare, honey," he murmurs at the customs lady who, smiling, waves us through.

Thence to check-in for our flight to Exuma. Here the security staff are equally worried by the size of Habu and also, it seems, the possibility that he might be some sort of 'mule'. For, apparently, the rule is that he will not only have to pass through the X-ray detector "door" but he will have to do it on his own, walking. Even given our immense pride in his abilities we are not too sure about this. L goes first while I hold him at heel: when she is ready I give the command "sit and stay". This he does with immaculate precision but he watches us with the unwinking stare of the hypnotist while the officials peep out from behind the safety of their counter: when they give the go ahead, on command from L he walks imperiously through the door to us for a cuddle and confirmation that he is not going to have to do any more of this flying lark on his own.

Various, small, island hopper airlines make the trip to Exuma including Pineapple Air and Calypso Air but we have chosen

Flamingo Air having previously struck an attractive deal to move the "circus". A slight problem presents itself when the check-in girl spots the kennel: it is too large to fit in the aircraft with the three of us and the pilot. This is soon resolved when another carrier, Sky Bahamas (who don't take large dogs) sportingly agree to bring it down on their scheduled flight, and without charge. So we march onto the tarmac and over to what looks like a model of the real thing—but no, this is what we are boarding. Access is up two stairs, over the wing and through a cockpit window. The big Bahamian pilot has boarded first and his eyes widen in a paroxysm of fear as Habu, keen not to be left behind, bounces smartly into the front seat of the plane and vaults over him into the rear "I not used to dem big dogs" he mumbles. We take our seats, the window is closed, the pilot mutters something unintelligible to the tower and off we taxi, abruptly becoming airborne.

We fly down to Exuma at 9000 feet, weaving between great aerial castles of cumulo nimbus cloud and with a stunning view of the myriad little tropical islands, surrounded by gin-clear tropical sea, that are the Exuma Cays, over a hundred miles in length, and visible from outer space. As we reduce height to 1500 feet for landing Habu suddenly expresses an interest in the outside world and decides to take a look out of the window. I watch as he peers in incomprehension first to one side then the other dotting the glass with his nose each time, as a kaleidoscope of land, jungle and sea rushes past underneath. Perplexed, he falls back onto the seat and, I swear, puts his paws over his eyes in disbelief. Landing, we taxi up to the charming little terminal. The building is constructed in classic Bahamian style with breezeblocks painted yellow and an asphalt shingle roof decorated in white elastic paint to deflect the sun and glue the shingles on. The whole is just, and only just, long enough to bear the painted legend "Exuma International Airport", a mild delusion of grandeur but excusable as flights do come in from Florida. Emerging from the customs room we are met by our beaming friends Peter (he of the NFU advertisement) and his wife Trish who, having persuaded us to choose this spot, promised to be here on our arrival to welcome us—and celebrate our first moments as residents of the Bahamian island of Exuma. They take photos of us outside the arrivals wire gate, with piles of cases and Habu, looking happy but weary and then, allaying our unfounded fears of potential problems at the house, drive us there for the first night of our new lives.

We have electricity and water—eureka! Our new bed and pillows are where we left them in our bedroom awaiting some sheets and us. In our "great room," as the Americans call it, is an enormous heap of sundry furniture and other necessities which we have bought in Miami on a previous trip and had shipped down in advance. It covers three quarters of the room and is over six feet high at its apex with trailers of bubble wrap, cardboard packaging and other miscellaneous pieces of flotsam riffling around its circumference. We had intended that Habu should sleep in here but take pity on the poor beast and put his dog bed in our bedroom. Suddenly overcome with exhaustion, we collapse into bed deciding that unpacking can start with the new day.

CHAPTER 3

The next morning we arise to carry out a detailed inspection of the new home. Although we did this on a visit a short time previously a number of "snagging items" were incomplete and we now need to see whether we really are free of builders.

We designed the house so that the three bedrooms and the great room have French windows which open out onto the main verandah and the sea beyond. The house is 75 feet across the garden from the water's edge and built on stilts so that we are 15 feet above sea level which, more by good luck than good judgement, gives impressive views to the east and south of the sheltering reefs and maritime traffic sailing into and out of George Town. This is important to avoid what we christened "empty sea syndrome"—looking at a deserted ocean—which is fine if you are on honeymoon! Tropical sunrises are striking. (When we bought the land it was virgin territory and the only way we could tell what the views might be like was to stand on the bonnet of our realtor's four wheel drive and peer over the jungle towards the sea). Externally, the house is painted pale turquoise to match the water of the bay beyond, with a white shingled roof to deflect the sun. Verandah balustrading and railings, door frames, window frames and concrete stilt supports are also painted white.

Internally the walls are white and the floors are all tiled to reduce the heat—white in the great room and pale terra cotta elsewhere. The ensuite bathrooms for the bedrooms and the utility room all lie along the back wall on the land side, as do the porch, stairs, and front door. The main verandah is 12 feet deep, covered and some 58 feet long and joins the south verandah which is 6 feet deep because we felt that it would be less likely to be regularly used. Although the house is single storey the ceilings are traditional Bahamian 'pickled' wood (painted with a thin glaze of white to allow the colour and grain of the timber to show through) known as "trays" so that there is plenty of height to keep the rooms cool. All the main rooms have air conditioning but a pleasant surprise is that because of the position a gentle, refreshing sea breeze wafts down the verandah, which is in shade by lunchtime and, as all the windows have been placed 'fore and aft,' provides natural ventilation throughout. Consequently, the air conditioning is virtually superfluous and even in high summer we will be kept sufficiently cool almost all of the time by the ceiling fans, if needed. The great room is so called, we believe, because it includes dining, kitchen and sitting areas all in the one space and is the only room which runs from the front to the back of the house with doors off to the bedrooms on either side.

There is plenty of snagging left to be done; for example we have no surfaces on the kitchen units and, indeed, it will be a further four months before we get rid of the tradesmen. Of particular note is the shower head in our bathroom. This high tech contrivance is intended to be a combined rainwater shower for that tropical downpour sensation combined with a hand held nozzle to do the business with those more inaccessible parts of the anatomy. The level of installation expertise required to instal such a wonder has been way beyond the ability of the sub-contracted plumber engaged. The best we ever wring out of the rainwater end is a Saharan trickle until one evening when I am sloughing off the grime of a day's indolence there is a slightly weary groan followed by a metallic crash and the whole edifice snaps off, the piping catching me a sharp blow as it collides with my head on its way down, plummeting to the floor and striking me fiercely on the toe. One feels very exposed when being chastised by recalcitrant equipment whilst naked and expletives come fluently to mind. Fortunately, the impact on the shower's performance is negligible—at least the hand nozzle continues to perform in its usual way and we plug the trickle escaping from the sheared-off pipe end where the rainwater shower isn't any more.

We connect our new American fridge-freezer and for several nights sleep is frequently interrupted by salvoes of loud reports as the freezer has phantom pregnancies making ice. Mercifully, this process stops when the ice bin reaches 'full'.

CHAPTER 4

The island is not for everyone—there are no race tracks, football stadia, rivers, mountains, theatres, cinemas, or shops selling what you need when you need it. It has been said that "Exuma sounds like a contented sigh"—or a swiftly deflating car tyre, depending on your frame of mind at the time.

ooooooooOooooooooo

Some little while after we arrive and our misdirected belongings have been reunited with us by our hopeless 'international' removals firm we unpack to find that amongst other unsolicited flotsam and jetsam three of our best, thickest woollen blankets. What use are they here in the Bahamas? Should we return them to the UK? We decide to sell them and in January post notices on the boards in the local supermarkets. In due course I am approached in the street by a Bahamian who looks like something out of a spaghetti western—black jeans and shirt with a leather bad hat and a large knife in his belt. I am mildly nervous, being new to the islanders' ways—he does look vaguely menacing and he is definitely looking at me! But it turns out he merely wants to enquire about the advertisement. (How he knows that I am the author of this masterpiece of marketing is a mystery.) Yes, we still have them and I will show them to him. He is OK with the price but then returns to say, "I can't take any, man—my girlfriend says they won't go with our bedroom colour scheme!" In early February when the temperature has plummeted to, for a Bahamian, an arctic 70° our man returns and, suitably chastened, takes the lot!

ooooooooOooooooooo

Today, we drive to George Town as usual, to deposit the rubbish—trash as it is called here and to commence trade discussions with Customs about five drums of elastic roof paint which we have imported from Miami. (There seems to be a failure on their part to accept the fact that if there were any drugs they would be exported from Exuma to the States rather than the other way round . . . . and a mutual understanding needs to be achieved). Driving through the Napa shop bend where a new enlarged store is being built it becomes apparent that enthusiasm for the build has included demolishing the right hand side of the cutting through which the Queen's Highway passes. The Bahamian Highway Code has been immeasurably improved by the addition of that well known international sign where a man floats an old red striped shirt on a wobbly stick in an indeterminate direction in the interests of guiding the traffic through a single lane obstruction. The result, predictably, is that traffic from both directions gleefully accepts its right of priority and so we find ourselves taking Hobson's choice between running aground on some evil spikes of limestone lying along the roadside or being mashed by a large, smelly, diesel truck with a load of gravel for one of the construction sites. I have discovered a number of ways of achieving sweaty palms and this is definitely one of them.

On arrival, we discover that George Town has been saved, albeit temporarily, from one of the more fey decisions of the Bahamian bureaucracy, namely, to close the 16 foot bridge in the town centre which allows the one way system to proceed in a more or less orderly fashion round the Victoria pond: this, with the notable exception of "les plus grands camions" with containers attached (from the supply ships) which are too big for it and hence ignore the system, travelling against the flow with air-horns blaring straight at the oncoming traffic with stimulating results. The other more telling effect from our point of view is that, with the closing of the bridge, our small and newly acquired boat would have been marooned in the local boatyards together with everyone else's; so would Exuma's entire supply of tourist hire boats. And access from the sea to shops and chandleries for the some 300 yachts moored in Queen Elizabeth Harbour would have been denied for two months during the peak tourist season—a positive howitzer shell in the foot for the Bahamas Tourist Board. But this proves just to be a postponement of intent and this particular insanity is eventually perpetrated, albeit later, in the spring when most of the tourists and boaters have left for the summer.

CHAPTER 5

Tonight we are going out for a meal to a restaurant at the north (extravagant) end of the island, next to the Four Seasons hotel and on the Emerald Bay marina beside the Yacht Club—very chi chi. The restaurant is called Wahoo, (which is a type of fish), for no apparent reason. Wahoo is not on the menu. The evening is like a warm blanket and we are met by a blast of air conditioning when we enter. Décor is best described as "Stokers Canteen, SS Titanic". Grey metal abounds and a certain feeling of lassitude pervades the atmosphere—lighting is certainly steerage. Nevertheless, the food is good and the wine is reasonably priced, for Exuma. We start with a round of conch fritters which have plenty of conch and good crisp batter. Main courses are chosen and include an international choice of steaks, which will be good coming from the States, chicken in various guises and fish including Red Snapper and Grouper fingers in batter. Service is brisk once decisions have been made and communicated to the staff. They are keen to clear up and go home by 8.30pm, or sooner, if at all possible. It is not a late evening. We are somewhat nonplussed at finding ourselves on the pavement all 'done and dusted' at this stage—never mind young, the night is virtually premature—but perhaps another time . . . .

ooooooooOooooooooo

Soon after our arrival on Exuma the election of the US president reaches fever pitch, even on our little island in the Bahamas mostly, we think, as a matter of brotherhood rather than nationality. The media tells us that a number of social and society events have been arranged in Washington for the great day. On the cusp of the Obama (another Irish president?) inauguration and celebratory parties we are glued to the TV set and my cup of joy o'er flows when, suddenly, along the bottom of the screen scrolls the breaking news, "Follow the inaugural balls from 9pm until midnight!"

oooooooo0oooooooo

There are a number of heavy jobs to do around the house mostly involving moving large quantities of rock, stones and soil. I am reflecting on this to our friend Peter who opines that what I need is a Hayshun for a couple of days. Knowing that we have imported L's pride and joy, her vastly expensive Hayter lawn mower to cut the lawns we shall lay, I ask him where I might hire such a machine. He gives me a pitying look and says, "A Haitian comes from Haiti and is an illegal immigrant costing $60 a day." Suitably crushed I discover that they may be hired at the hiring fair outside the Silver Dollar restaurant and bar, a watering-hole for the locals on the outskirts of George Town. As one can also receive a $5000 on-the-spot fine from Immigration for employing such a person and lose one's visitors visa instantly, I decide to use alternative methods and invest in a shovel and pickaxe.

In the following weeks, I muse on the irony that despite my mature years I'm only now being introduced to the delights of "the pickaxe school of gardening". Although the soil is fertile, because ours is a virgin site and previously uncultivated, the land is liberally sewn with stones varying in size from gravel pebbles through fists to monsters that I can only swivel rather than lift.

These last are so large that they have to be rolled and manhandled into the wheelbarrow with it lying on its side. The barrow is then levered back upright and I totter it to the stone's new desired location which is mostly at the end of what we intend to be our lawn. A spade is useless on this heavily stoned terrain and the pickaxe is essential; the sod must be broken with an awl rather than a chisel. Given the heat which is thrown off the bare soil, two fresh dry tee shirts a day are more than useful. Some weeks later after losing half a stone and having found muscles that I didn't know I had, the lawn area is rid of stones and ready for turf and I am building a dry stone wall along its boundary from the attractive white limestone that I have harvested. Dry stone walling seems similar to a three dimensional jigsaw puzzle and is a harmless, satisfying, very absorbing and healthy pursuit! One does need to be tolerably light fingered, however, as stories about castrating camels with bricks come to mind.

ooooooooOoooooooo

It is late afternoon and I am doing some chores in the shade on our main verandah. Cooled by a soft breeze, I pause momentarily to admire the stunning view as the early evening sun paints the sea of Queen Elizabeth harbour bright turquoise on its way to lighting up the vibrant greens of Stocking Island. Stocking is virtually uninhabited but as my eyes focus I see what appears to be a substantial apartment block moving along it at a sedate 6 miles an hour followed by a single mast some 80 feet behind. Initially, I am at a loss. Then the hallucination resolves itself: I decide I can guess what it is and, sure enough, when it reaches a low stretch of the island all is revealed as the massive upper decks of a super-yacht with, 80 feet aft of the bridge, a complete 35 foot sailing sloop lashed to the stern deck. It is none other than "Le Grand Bleu," one of the 6 largest private yachts in the world and until recently belonged to one Mr Abramovich. It is now a cast-off according to the internet, having been given by Mr A to a friend, and is presently cruising the Caribbean.

oooooooo0oooooooo

Although we know a number of folk on the island from our researching and house-building visits, we are still finding our way socially so we have invited our new American neighbours Terry and Dorothy Mildenberg to come round and check over the house—or rather, charmingly, they have invited themselves. It is 12.30 and so wine or a Kalik beer is offered. This local brew is a type of lager and is the staple beer of the Bahamas. He will have a red and she will have a Club Soda as sobriety is required for a high level bridge match at two pm. They have kindly brought a small carrot cake as a hello offering—even though we and many others went to their house at five pm sharp yesterday for a "quick cocktail" which went on forever mainly because the G and Ts were so strong that one became quite incoherent and thus it took some considerable time to say goodbye in a comprehensible manner. The cake, unintentionally, takes the form of a small War of Independence monitor warship with two masts, the tips of which are painted touch-paper cerulean blue, leading one to suspect the presence of an ominous incendiary device: we shall see. Nevertheless, it proves delicious.

Today is our second American cocktail party this week, again starting at 5pm. L is hurrying back from tea at 3 with the Tourist Board and a number of other ladies who are new(ish) residents on the island—a sort of induction ceremony. This will free me to walk along the beach and empty the dog before our hasty departure for drinks. One begins to comprehend why the yanks go to bed so early: those that do drink start at 5 and have achieved oblivion by 8.30. Those that don't should have done.

CHAPTER 6

Minns (Watersports) boatyard on Victoria Pond

Down at Minns' boatyard on Victoria Pond, the small land-locked, sea water lake in George Town, is a dilapidated ramshackle hut which is the workshop lair of the 'boys' who repair and maintain the island's leisure boats. Head of this colourful rogues' gallery is the magnificent Jay who looks like an amiable Silverback and has a voice to match with the timbre of an ocean liner's foghorn. Whilst the effect is reinforced by his lower torso and legs which are covered by what looks like a blacksmith's apron, perched on top of this majestic specimen of alpha male-hood sits an incongruously petite piece of headgear to shade him from the strong sun—a dainty little straw hat with a band of delicate artificial roses arranged artfully around its base. The words 'pea' and 'elephant' come to mind. But the gargantuan Jay rumbles round the wooden jetties blissfully unaware of the abiding contrasts of his appearance.

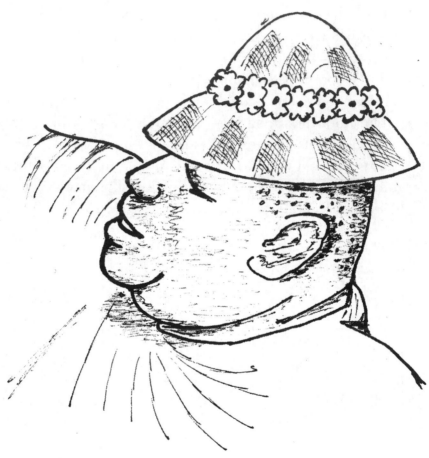

Jay's hat

He is, however, an excellent mechanic, which will be invaluable to us for we know nothing of marine engines and have bought a boat because to be without one on the island is like trying to play a clarinet with one hand. The boat is about 18 feet long with an outboard motor and will take five people, or four people and a decent sized dog. Before we leave for a short trip to the UK we ask the boatyard to haul it and generally service it so that it will be ready for us after the end of the hurricane season. On our return we find that it has already been put back into the water so we decide with ill-restrained excitement to take it out and trial it. Our outward voyage to Stocking Island is uneventful although we note that, strangely, the stern scupper vents have corks bunged in them.

Our picnic lunch is preceded by a swim and afterwards by a walk during which we comment frivolously that clouds are beginning to gather. Alarmed by the speed at which they are coming up we agree to return to George Town and swiftly pack the boat. Switching on the engine, we spot that the boat is low in the water and indeed the dive ladder shelf at the stern is at water level, several inches below normal. As we start off gingerly the heavens open and tip out a full-blooded tropical stair-rod shower. Whilst the "Bimini' shelter keeps the rain off us it is bucketing into the boat but there is no sign of the bilge pump working. The consensus is that we should return without delay and so I throttle up. Immediately, the boat raises its bow out of the sea like Jaws sniffing blood and digs in the engine at the back. And a wall of water made by our own wake cascades in over the stern. This is a very bad idea! We slow right down and L starts to bail with our small plastic picnic box. Whoever said that it was better to travel hopefully than to arrive was well wide of the mark. Half an hour later and greatly relieved we struggle to our slip on the boatyard jetty. One of the staff brings a pump and battery and we open the bilge hatch. The bilge is completely full of water which takes three hours to pump out. We ask them to check the bilge pump in the morning and leave for home bedraggled, chastened and cold for warm showers, dry clothes and shelter.

CHAPTER 7

Binning mountains of bubblewrap and despatching the 'furniture pyramid' in the living room has finally been successfully achieved but we now realise that a variety of essentials have been excluded from our initial inventory. Accordingly, we have gone to Miami to buy furniture and household equipment because it is a fraction of the price it would cost in the Bahamas, even allowing for shipping and duty. We are staying for three days so have employed a driver to navigate through the horrific traffic and tell us where we need to go. He is a French-Canadian illegal (we subsequently discover) called André who meets us at the airport, a slim voluble fellow with a modern minimal "Guy Fawkes" moustache and beard, dressed in tee shirt, shorts and flip-flops. Speaking American at machine gun speed with a strong French accent he is charming but almost unintelligible and takes us to our hotel to settle in for a night's sleep before the shop fest onslaught of the morrow.

As we soon discover, he drives like a Frenchman on the Paris pérepherique. After an early, hasty breakfast on day one we leave the hotel and are soon racing along the Miami State highway in a mad life-size scalextric game where rival lunatics fling themselves onto and off it crossing lanes completely randomly. As André's enthusiasm for the task in hand mounts so does our speed until at 70 mile per hour and fever pitch, he removes both hands from the steering wheel the better to gesticulate and starts steering the car with his knees yelling all the while (the windows are wide open because the air conditioning is long gone), "We do this, we do that, tac, tac, tac!" It is terrifying.

We visit a kaleidoscope of "stores" including Home Depot (pronounced deepoh), J C Penny, Best Buy, Office Depot, Petsmart, Crate and Barrel, Pottery Barn (which does not sell pots) and Walmart. The day passes in a blur and we are deposited damp and wrung out at our hotel 8 hours after starting. But we have bought all manner of things including cushions, linen, a barbecue, cooker, electric razor, standby electric generator and the smallest television in Christendom. In my view we'll go cross-eyed or need opera glasses to see anything on it but it is certainly miniscule, wall mounted and looks like a disengaged microwave door so it is very tidy and will not be intrusive (we will probably forget it is there; after all, out of sight is out of mind, unless, of course, we want a quick burger.)

That evening we eat out well at a beach promenade restaurant and are serenaded by a live blues band who encourage requests from the customers. Feeling mellow and nostalgic I ask the big old black bluesman playing lead guitar if they will play Booker T"s classic "Green Onions" he beams "Sure!" but only half the band know it—the rest are too young. After a huddle discussing chord sequences they break into it and do three verses spot on, the keyboards player rising well to Booker T's standards. My day is complete. So, the following day the trip is declared a success and we return to Exuma happily shopped out. The tiny TV has proved to be a great talking point amongst friends, a source of their endless amusement and we have suffered much ribaldry as a result. But that's OK; we can watch the tennis on it—with a magnifying glass.

CHAPTER 8

I's cousin and her husband, Anne and Jim are coming to stay on their way to a new life in the States having sold up and fled the UK. On the day of arrival, our Pajero does its thing and throws one of its intermittent break downs. Being resourceful, we have acquired a little Kia as back-up for these eventualities and having re-started the Pajero we head for the airport in both cars, just in case. The plane is a small Sky Bahamas charter and, uncharacteristically, it arrives late.

Usually Sky is notorious for leaving when "all the passengers are on board" so departure time is flexible and can be a good twenty minutes early. Moreover, the passenger list can be extremely casual to the extent that on one occasion a friend who had checked in was relaxing in Kermit's Airport Lounge and Bar (no, really!); hearing the sound of propellers revving, the slow realisation dawned to his horror that take off was imminent. Racing onto the tarmac, he gesticulated at an airport employee who managed to attract the pilot's attention and the flight was held while the cabin steps were re-lowered for his breathless embarkation.

Jim and Anne step off the late flight and into a tropical cloudburst. The weather has been atrocious and there has been flooding in some parts of the island. However, they are bombed out and seem cheerfully to accept that this is just another experience in their new lives: Jim is a stout, piratical fellow with a full short white beard and a sense of humour but missing the bandanna and the eye-patch. Anne is attractively long-suffering. At any rate they both are glad to be here and appreciative of the warmth. Jim announces that as the flight decelerated down the tarmac one of the plane's brakes seized and so instead of turning 180° to enter the apron it executed a smart 360°. The airport fire engine (one of two in working order on the island) was standing by to add to the torrents of water deluging from the heavens but was not needed. We return home without mishap or breakdown and are relieved not to face the prospect of spending the bank holiday shoe-horned into the little Kia.

As the rains continue we constantly revise our guest plan as more and more fine weather activities become inappropriate. Luckily Jim and Anne like swimming and snoozing, neither of which is precluded by the downpour and both of which are encouraged by the temperature. One day, we take them shopping with the idea that they will cook supper to keep everyone on their toes. At our end of the island there are four small supermarkets. Frequently it is necessary to visit all four to fill the shopping basket with the goods on one's list; this might sound like diversity but is more a question of who still has some of the product needed in stock. For sure, in Exuma the path to eating a successful supper is to see what you can buy and fit it to a recipe rather than the other way round.

Deciding to shop with a menu in mind is a frustration waiting to happen. They end up finding the ingredients they are looking for and announce that they will cook something that sounds suspiciously like "sopa de putana". I assume that I am going slightly deaf but this turns out to be fairly near the truth. Jim announces with gusto and a gleam in his eye that it is "spaghetti putane" and is traditionally used after a hard winter's evening at the office by the ladies of the night in Naples to keep themselves warm. I forebear to ask him, in front of Anne, how he knows this. Anyway, it is a spectacular concoction full of anchovies, black olives, chillies, feta cheese and garlic to name only some of the more discernable ingredients. It slips down a treat.

ooooooooOooooooooo

Drinking a "Goombay Smash" is a right of passage for all visitors to Exuma and there is no more appropriate place to do it than sitting back in Adirondack chairs after a hot day on the beach dandling ones feet in the ocean on a balmy early evening at Chat n' Chill, a beach bar and restaurant on Stocking Island facing across the Queen Elizabeth harbour to Exuma. These drinks are a concoction of rum, coconut rum, pineapple juice, orange juice and grenadine. For one dollar more an additional shot of rum is added—essential to the moment. They are deceptively mild and 'more-ish' because of the fruit juices and usually catch the unwary by surprise particularly as visitors seem to be somehow hard-wired into saying, "I think I'll just have another one of those," and another, and another . . . . Indeed, Giles Vardy, a guest of our good friends Simon and Cynthia Johnson became so 'refreshed,' as he later described it, that he fell into a deep slumber so relaxed that when he awoke his teenage boys had succeeded in nail varnishing all his toes bright vermillion.

On another occasion, showing acquaintances John and Linda round the Harbour we have reached the Goombay stage when we suddenly remember that their taxi is booked for 5pm. John tries, without success to raise the taxi driver's cellphone from his Blackberry and finally we ask the girl behind the bar if she can contact him—no problem. "Hey Patrick!" She booms—Bahamas phone calls render telephonic assistance entirely superfluous.

"Where you is?" "You in de P and P?" "We got your ride heah,—yeah, dey drinkin' Goombay Smashes on de beach, but soon reach—yeah man!" Then to us, "He OK." she says.—relief all round.

CHAPTER 9

April is the month when everything on Exuma stops for ten days, effectively, for Regatta. Specifically, this is the National Bahamas Family Islands Regatta and is the final of all the sailing heats that have previously taken place throughout the islands during the course of the year. Every carrier lays on extra flights to and from Nassau to George Town and all accommodation on the island is booked solid as competitors, supporters and fans converge on the island from throughout the Bahamas. Nassau police lend the local constabulary additional motor bikes and drivers to supplement the two on the island and the ferries plying the route down from the capital are full of cars, "expat" Exumans and others. Even the local shipping carriers enter into the spirit, transporting the competitors' sloops on their supply ships from the various other islands down to Exuma. Meanwhile a shanty town of shacks selling everything from booze to breakfasts springs up on the mole of the government dock accompanied by humungous sound systems which, apart from adding to the festivities, play island music loud enough to jolt ones intestines and make a skeleton jive.

The races are held in Elizabeth Harbour, which, because it is a body of water some five miles long by a mile a wide that is protected on two sides, offers a world class sailing venue. The race programme is a moveable feast depending largely on when all the boats and crews have assembled. This year we wanted to watch a race from the shore. (A better way is to watch it from a friend's boat as one is much closer to the action and the piratical mayhem instilled in others by the rum, excitement and adrenalin of skippering a powerful speed boat in tempestuous waters will be visited by them on your friend's craft rather than yours). Feeling that the Tourist Board would be the logical place to discover the race times, I give them a ring having already seen a race start at 8.30am in the distance. "What races are on today?"

"There's only one and it starts at 9am." (er . . . . no, clearly not!) We subsequently watch a "B" class race which starts at 12.30.

Competition is between the beautiful Bahamian sloops "A", "B", and "C' class depending on size. These wooden boats are based on the old Bahamian work boats but are now built for competition. As there is no limit on mast height, only on hull length, many of these boats are "over-rigged" which gives them spectacular sail square footage and makes for an awe-inspiring sight when they are sailing with all the stops out. For this reason, some of the "A: class boats, although only 28 feet long, will have as many as fifteen crew, most of who's purpose is ballast. Their job is to "trapeze"—shinning out along the two 10 foot planks of timber that are slung out over the sides after one end has been locked in the footings on the deck. Once out, they all sit in a long, precarious, line like so many pelicans on each plank until the time comes to tack. At this point they all scramble back inboard, uproot the planks and, ramming them into the footings on the opposite side, sling them outboard before leaping along them to seaward again. Astonishingly, we have only ever seen one instance of "man overboard" arising from these antics, a sure testament to the agility of the Bahamian crews. Despite converting to international sailing racing rules in 2006 (The rules say that a late boat is disqualified.) the start time is still Bahamian and can differ by as much as two hours from that indicated in the programme so ensuring that all the boats are present and ready to race.

The start is exhilarating to watch. All fifteen competing finalist boats from across the Bahamas are lined up head to wind on anchor with the sails down. They are given a one minute gun and at the crack of the starting gun sails are raised and the anchors hauled in with all speed. From then on it is "who dares wins" as the skippers indulge in some spectacular carve ups to gain wind and shave time. One regulation that is upheld is the requirement that all boats end the race with the same number of crew that they started with in order to stop any "walking the plank" to lighten the load on the last leg. Inevitably, there is the occasional capsize but the waters are shallow enough for the boat's ballast, usually stones, to be extracted the following morning and for the "wreck" to be re-floated without damage.

On the Saturday afternoon after the last race has been won the final party is officially opened when the Royal Bahamas Police Marching Band, resplendent in brilliant white jackets, red belt and navy trousers with wide red stripes down the seams, gives a charming and disciplined performance along the road outside the Government Administration building; the prizes for the race winners are awarded (a long and complex process) and festivities rev up with the Police Pop Band which is the rump of the main Police Band playing a series of local calypsos with devastating accuracy and speed for 45 minutes. By now "the joint is jumping" and the party reaches a crescendo; bands, calypso, disco, noise, dancing, drinking and beaming, sweaty, joyous face are everywhere with everyone enjoying themselves as only the Bahamians can. The Peace and Plenty hotel bars are so crammed that there is no room for wrists, let alone elbows and the party goes on all night until the last reveller drops. The members of the Police Band spend their habitual night on the floor of the Exuma Resource Centre building.

The next morning the silence in George Town is eerie. By mid morning the shacks are being torn down and are nearly demolished. But the chaos has moved on to the airport which is now a scene from Bedlam with its dodgy air conditioning as a plague of weary revellers tries single-mindedly to escape from the island and be back at work, wherever, for the following morning. Noise levels are stratospheric, tempers are frayed and hangovers are deeply painful. The mass of humanity surges towards the departure gate every time an outbound flight is announced and frustration mounts as only limited quantities of people can leave at a time. Nobody in their right mind flies on this Sunday unless they absolutely have to.

Overall, the regatta costs some $250,000. It is difficult to assess whether this represents value for money but it is certainly good public relations for the tourist industry, the main source of revenue for the island and is a 'helluva' party!

ooooooooOoooooooo

As it is the End of Regatta—there are shortages of everything on the island even the most unexpected produce—but salvation is at hand; the container ship appears and runs smartly aground opposite our house on a sand bank in the channel through Elizabeth Harbour to George Town. All that we want is probably on that boat and there it stays as we sit on our verandah and contemplate it, tantalisingly within sight but out of reach for two days.

Driving into George Town to shop there is great excitement for us as a feral Peacock meanders across the road in front of us. We know that they live at the north end of the island but had not expected to see one down here. Having kept them in the UK it is like seeing an old friend out of context. Almost by way of fraternal greeting it spreads its tail feathers and displays—a five foot fan, a quivering mirage of blues, golds and turquoises, a stunning example of the beauty of nature.

In the town centre Exuma Markets, one of our four "supermarkets" has a new manager named Phil. As he reorganizes the whole shop all the products appear in confusingly different places and, suddenly, there seems to be much less stock. We re-christen him Phil the Shelves. This is a mildly childish pastime but gives us much (mainly) innocent pleasure. The whole island appears to have run out of basic supplies including milk, tonic water, Gordon's gin and diet coke and myriad other daily essentials too trivial to mention (dental floss?). Given that Regatta occurs every year at the same time, rather like Christmas, it is a considerable mystery that the revellers manage to denude the island's supermarkets without a whimper, never mind a fight (what can they do with all the dental floss?). Worst of all, it encourages a siege mentality so that people will buy 30 loo rolls just because they are in stock which, of course, exacerbates the whole process. We know this to be a fact because residents have shown us their loo roll mountains with pride.

CHAPTER 10

On this island there are, as yet, no drink driving laws. It has to be said that being faced by an oncoming speeding police car or local pickup it is easy to see why: driving here whilst sober requires award-winning bravery.

There is no breathalyser on Exuma and the authorities take a relaxed view of drink driving. That is, they don't mind drink driving, as such, but become unhappy with folk who drink while actually driving. Around this spring time of year the sap rises even more that usual in the Bahamians and the weekends are an opportunity for some serious alcohol consumption. This coupled with Regatta or the Junkanoo summer festival makes for Herculean efforts to party which create a fairly convivial atmosphere most Friday and Saturday nights especially as the seductively sultry evenings inflame a vigorous thirst. A hobby of mine is to note the numbers of abandoned cars along the couple of miles journey as I take Habu for his walk first thing on Sunday morning. Today is a three vehicle carnage day; one is in the roadside ditch, the second, a deserted van, is slewed across someone's drive totally blocking the entrance and the last, improbably, seems to have come to rest 4 feet up in a tree. I am lost in admiration, not only for the sheer ingenuity of the drivers, but also for their ability to escape from these accidents completely unscathed. We are assured that the reason for this is that they are so inebriated that they are totally relaxed and survive these crashes pretty much without injury.

oooooooo0oooooooo

On our way into George Town to shop for supplies we pass by, or more accurately, through Palm Bay Beach Club. This started out as a small cluster of thoughtfully positioned single storey clapboard cottages in turquoise, cerulean blue, rust red and cadmium yellow, all with views of the beach and ocean. It is now a sprawling development covering the hill inland of the road, as well. The houses now boast two floors, some set out as apartments and sit in rows cheek by jowl. All have wooden verandahs and balustrades. I have nicknamed it Dodge City. Whenever we pass I expect to see horses drawn up and hitched to the rails in front, a volley of gunfire to erupt as doors and windows are simultaneously shattered by corpses cannoning out through them, and a flinty-eyed hero to emerge from the bar-restaurant with two smoking sixguns and a whiff of cheroot. This state of affairs will have arisen because whatever is ordered from the bar/restaurant menu is, traditionally, quite likely to be "off" that day.

In some respects Great Exuma is quite like one imagines the Wild West to have been. Apart from attracting genuine tourists, the investment potential acts as a magnet for every type of "developer," card sharp, snake oil salesman, horse-thief, gunslinger, villain and rogue. All are washed up on the shores at the airport and drift through the island telling the locals of their grandiose and wondrous plans, often as multitudinous as the tattoos on their arms, torso, legs and every exposed piece of their anatomy and undoubtedly more besides. These schemes surface freely from shaven-headed enthusiasts in the George Town bars and evaporate just as freely a few days later when their authors leave the island at the end of their holidays; the locals smile, nodding sagely, waiting for the next extravaganza to unfold.

oooooooooOooooooooo

St. Andrew church from Victoria Pond

In the centre of George Town, four-square between the quaint Peace and Plenty hotel and the little Straw Market which sells crockery, straw hats, tee shirts and trinkets lies the Administration building, a charming structure with pleasing proportions painted in a pale pink wash with a small portico supported by white pillars. In its right wing is housed the Magistrates Court and the Police Station. An impressive sign sits above the latter, "Divisional Headquarters for Exuma and Ragged Island District, George Town Police Station." Underneath all this magnificence hangs an endearingly old-fashioned, not to say iconic, original Blue Lamp with "POLICE" written into the glass on all four sides. This colonial relic would bring a tear to many a hoary old retired village 'bobby' in rural villages across the U.K. and is a reminder that the islands only attained independence from Britain in 1973. Even now much of the legislature is still British based and English common law forms the basis of the Bahamian judicial system. Ultimately, an appeal from the Bahamas Court of Appeal still goes to the judicial committee of the Privy Council in England.

Also in the centre of town sits St Andrew's church, a pretty whitewashed building with blue gothic shutters, perched on high ground overlooking the Victoria Pond and Minns' boatyard. Here during the service certain Bahamian ladies dressed spectacularly in Sunday best, as for a day at the races, get irreverent giggles when the pastor is carried away by her own enthusiastic verbosity, the humour in the sermon being entirely unintentional.

CHAPTER 11

Until recently Habu has been a coconut fanatic. That is to say he searches them out and then shakes them until he has wrenched off the matting husk leaving the kernel. This is a perfect sphere and represents a good ball substitute if he can persuade us humans to throw it into the sea for him. Wise folk stand well aside from this event as much splashing, frolicking and swimming ensues before the coconut is returned to the shore. We also use the coconut to get him off our boat and onto the sand, an even wetter experience as L throws and I am usually holding the boat by the stern for disembarking. Habu takes a running leap and launches himself from the stern into the sea beside me with tsunami results lending new meaning to the phrase 'a quick dip'.

Nevertheless, there is a practical aspect to all this. Just occasionally when we are camped out on our own empty, apart from us, piece of paradise beach, tourists in a hire boat will see us anchored in the shallows and assume that if we can do it safely so can they. As they veer from 'passing by' mode to 'definitely steering towards us with intent to intrude' mode we unleash the doomsday machine. A coconut is hurled as far towards the oncoming interference as possible. With a shout of "fetch it Habu!" he erupts from the sand where he has been lying, probably unnoticed by the tourists and, flinging great sprays of the stuff around as he goes, leaps into the sea barking his head off with joy. Initially, he does a porpoise-run leap-frogging through the water throwing great sheets of it into the air each time he lands until he is out of his depth where he begins to swim with grim determination. Having 'saved' the coconut the process is repeated in reverse as he returns to dry land. Usually one application is sufficient for us to see the bows of the offending boat swing sharply out to sea as the occupants look for a quieter place to picnic. But if one is not enough, a second always does the trick.

However, while we keep a stock of coconuts on the boat they are now spurned on walks in favour of a new and more exhilarating sport, for Habu has become a crab-holer. Along the high tide line in the sand are many holes about one inch in diameter and roughly one in five is occupied by a little white beach crab the same size as the hole. Habu sniffs each hole and digs up any promising specimens although, in oil drilling parlance, a number are "dry". So far as we can tell these holes are hockey-stick shaped and the crab lurks at the end until loss of nerve obliges it to scuttle to the surface and make a bolt for the sea. Habu already has the wound of valour on his nose where he has been bitten en route. But the thrill of the chase is too strong and he dances round darting at the crab as it streaks for the safety of the ocean.

He is also useful as an attraction for other species. In the waters of Queen Elizabeth Harbour between Stocking Island and Exuma lives a family of dolphins. The male and female produce a baby each year and are often seen by various folk swimming and playing in the sea. As we motor across the bay Habu sits right on the bow of the boat peering forwards like a ship's figurehead. He acts as a magnet to the dolphins who are intrigued by his presence and come to play, sprinting along beside the boat and leaping in our wash. They are with us for nearly half an hour before they leave for other enjoyment. And we are filled with pleasure at having been chosen to witness this exuberant exhibition.

Turtles are also regular sightings in the harbour but they are quite shy and, as often as not, one only comes upon them foraging for food by surprise, sending them diving swiftly if the boat is too near. Varieties include leatherbacks, greens, and hawksbills.

ooooooooOooooooooo

And so to the dentist for a scale and polish. In order to get there one must pass through the government clinic car park where a pack of the staff's cars surround the island's sclerotic ambulance hemming it in most effectively. I arrive early and sit with a book in the shade of the clinic's verandah along with other supplicants. Finally, the nurse comes out, a magnificent Bahamian lady of middle years with bright blonde hair and a small jewel in her nose. She beams, "You for de doctor?" (All dentists are doctors, here, following the American pattern). "Come on in, he see you now." The island dentist is Bill Lee our friend and neighbour who lives in the pale pink house looking down on us from the hill immediately to our north. He is a tall slim man with a ready smile and a well-controlled grey beard. One is greeted by a, "Hi there, how'r ya doing. What's new?"

His surgery is in a room at the clinic on the outskirts of George Town and appointments are made by ringing up the great man himself between patients so that he can answer the phone and book you in on his laptop diary. It turns out that this is his most modern piece of equipment. The dentist's chair is old but fits OK and in the corner lurks an aged Xray machine nodding in the silence like an out-of-work Triffid. Its days of gainful activity are clearly over for on its upper arm hang Island Regatta burgees for the last eight years drooping languidly in sequence under a light patina of dust. It was originally painted a beguiling shade of pale green, presumably to match the mien of the patient. Beside the chair is a dental spittoon similarly coloured with its ceramic bowl around which water would usually swirl before plashing down the plughole. But here no waters swirl; instead the bowl contains a large handwritten notice which reads "DO NOT SPIT IN HERE—USE THE BASIN ON THE WALL." Bill wanders round imparting amiable island gossip mostly on the subject of who is doing what to whom while he pokes and thrusts at my teeth. Half an hour later, I am released from the chair having had, without doubt, the best scale and polish of my life. I pay my $40 fee and muse on the conundrum that Bill is clearly overrun in the winter when the boaters are here but has never put up his fees to balance supply with demand.

ooooooooOooooooo

Because today is time for a bit of admin—bills, banks, credit cards and such, I am on the computer in my august role as head of the family whilst my wife is doing some cooking. Unfortunately, I am death to equipment and can drop a photocopier at 20 paces: as usual, I am bamboozled by a minor technical problem but L, who is comfortable with her IT skills, comes to assist. In doing so, to my horror, she liberally sprays the keyboard with a fragrant melange of raw meat, garlic and onions thereby creating, in short order, another world first—the "computer burger". The dog has taken a sudden and profound interest in computing.

CHAPTER 12

John and Patricia are our first guests to the new house apart
from family so we view their arrival with excitement and a little
trepidation. Will they be bored, have the right clothing, like their
room, enjoy the food and so on. Patricia is an elegant honey
blonde with a guileless face, insatiable curiosity and an inability to
whisper to the extent of asking loud intimate questions all about
our neighbours while sitting on the verandah in full earshot.
John is "our man in Havana", cool as the proverbial cucumber
complete with immaculately creased trousers, lightweight jacket
and Panama hat. We have warned them that all we can offer is a
soft breeze on the verandah, a comfortable chair, a good book and
a rum punch; there is comparatively little 'professional' night life
or passeggiata; one makes one's own. However, we need not have
worried. A mock, terse order from John for "whatever I should be
drinking with rum in it" shortly after arrival bodes well and they
settle in quickly. It turns out that they spent holidays in Barbados
some years ago and so are not as green about the Tropics as we had
feared. Indeed, John quickly masters the local accent including
the "man" which tends to conclude most Bahamian sentences.

We ask them for a report on the guest facilities as our guinea
pigs and the list is refreshingly short: the bathroom door will not
close and lock and the Sun shines directly into the bedroom at
7am. We agree to adjust the Sun, slightly.

Habu has taken a paternal interest in John's well-being to the extent of lying beside his chair whenever he goes onto the verandah to read. John decides to swim off the house and goes in with his snorkel and goggles. Habu spots him some thirty-five yards out and, perceiving him to be unconscious, that is, floating face down with a small tube sticking out of the top of his head, bounds into the water intent on rescue. Refusing all commands to return to the shore he swims powerfully and purposefully to John who is entirely unaware of the unfolding drama. Habu commits his life saving coup de grace by leaping on the back of the unsuspecting John thereby nearly causing the very seizure which it is designed to avoid. John is quite unnerved by this attention and Habu refuses to leave him and return to the beach, nearly drowning John in the process. In the event, both return to the shore unharmed although John mutters "I thought I'd been hit by a speedboat at least!"

This evening we take our friends down island to see the sunset, driving to the low single carriageway bridge, called obscurely "the Ferry" which joins Great and Little Exuma. The location for this entertainment is the Peace and Plenty Bonefish Lodge hotel situated beside the Ferry and mainly patronised by addicted game fishermen. It is a beautifully peaceful, still evening and we are the only customers sitting on the hotel's wide, wooden jetty jutting out into the bay which is, in effect, a tidal lake as its entrance is so narrow. Later in the evening the owner of the hotel will turn on the jetty spotlights and feed the four foot lemon sharks who know that the lights mean supper. We sit talking quietly and drinking our "Bahama Mamas" a pint tumbler cocktail of rum, coconut rum, pineapple juice, grenadine and copious ice. By now the sea is a motionless flat mirror reflecting the sky in shades of the palest cerulean blue with hints of yellow. The sun is a ball of yellow and orange on the horizon and an osprey sweeps in over our heads making a low run across the still water. Two hundred yards out he suddenly swoops and cleanly lifts a large wriggling fish in both talons. Increasing his wing beats to carry the extra load he bears the trophy off to the bush for supper. As the sun slips below the horizon we rise to leave before the "no-see 'ems," sand flies, decide we are part of their food chain too. We head "up-island" into the warm embrace of a Caribbean evening and the promise of a convivial supper.

CHAPTER 13

Twice a week we play a mixed doubles tennis "mixer" with whoever turns up. When our American friend Don is on island he is a regular and acts as master of ceremonies because he lives in the gated community where the tennis club is situated. Don is a compact man with twinkly feet and he likes to win—none of that Brit "play the game" nonsense. The courts are hard and Don insists on new balls each session so their bounce is extreme which favours his game of high lobs, spins, flicks, volleys and serves. On this particular day we have an English downpour which would normally be enough to terminate an Exumian tennis session. However, to prove our mettle we decide to play on the wet courts as soon as the rain stops. As a result the new furry balls absorb the moisture from the surfaces and become "English"—fast, low and heavy. Intriguingly, Don's game deteriorates and becomes quite ordinary during this period whilst the rest of us maintain our usual performance levels.

Tennis is either played here between 7.30 and 9.30am or 3.30 and 5.00pm to avoid the heat. Unfortunately the courts have been designed to face north/south instead of East/West so there is no avoiding blinding sun when serving at the north end or receiving high lobs from the south end.

A constant battle of wills rages between the sulky manager of the estate and our "gang" of club members as he tries continually to encourage us to join mixers that he arranges at vast cost when, as paid up members we can all play for free. His approach seems to transmit itself to his female security staff on the entrance gate whose attitude could be best summed up as waspish. Unusually, however, there is sometimes a rare fleeting thaw.

"Trince is very bubbly today," L remarks on one such occasion.

"Mm, like an overripe septic tank," I mutter.

Mostly, I play singles "gentleman's tennis" with our friend Alexander and a civilised interlude in life it is. He is a pukka chap; his tennis kit is a slight update on Rod Laver's and could be classed as 'Public school' circa 1965 consisting of a tee shirt grey with age and washing, merging into long off-white uncreased baggy shorts. His feet are encased in short grey socks and genuine old plimsolls (I have a suspicion that he does not own a pair of 'trainers'). When we reach deuce which occurs frequently we don't have any of that dreadful "ad-in, ad-out' nonsense," it's "Advantage Carruthers" etc. Proper tennis.

On an island where one cannot buy an electric razor or a kitchen knife sharpener it is, of course, entirely possible to have one's tennis racquet restrung. One of the "boaters" living in the Harbour, "Dennis the tennis," performs this service without charge provided that a donation is made to the island's Bahamian tennis coach. This is to ensure compliance with the immigration laws that foreigners should not take jobs that could be performed by locals.

There is nowhere to buy tennis racquets on the island so L has purchased one from the United States. To her consternation, it arrives with no strings. Commenting on this she opines to Howard, our tennis partner, that it must be an Irish racquet. "No." He says "That's definitely a Bahamian one!"

CHAPTER 14

Recently, we have become concerned about our daughter Sophie's bedroom which seems to have a permanent, if invisible, guest. As she is only in residence for two weeks or so a year this is a worry. Evidence comes in the form of small dark brown turd pellets which look ominously like those of rats. However, there are no other signs to support this diagnosis—indeed the pellets have white tips on one end and, as often as not, seem to cling to the wall which is visual, messy and mystifying in equal measure. As our computer, telephone, internet connection and printer are all kept in this room we use it every day. But no sightings.

One day we need hard copies of some flight details, bookings and tickets so we turn the printer on. It does have some problems with the climate and the salt air, but all the lights flash reassuringly on its control panel, emitting a long grinding squeak as the photo mechanism slides juddering into place. Then, to our astonishment, an enormous pale brown gecko streaks out of it and up the wall hanging on hard with his circular suction footpads as he goes. He (or it may be a she—it's difficult to tell with geckos) stops five feet up and peers at us dolefully out of vast, round, limpid jet-black eyes, reproachful at having his sleep disturbed during daylight and rockets for cover behind the dressing table wall mirror. At last, the solution to our mystery! On subsequent occasions we pass him like ships in the day as he becomes more familiar with the fact that his warm and secure bedroom is our printer and we appreciate that he is our gecko in the machine.

Sometimes if we look down between the printer and the wall we can see his little back legs and tail hanging out—for him it's a given that if he cannot see us then he is totally incognito. On other occasions he'll sit down and peer at us, assuming that because it's darkish down there, he is invisible.

Nevertheless, diplomatic overtures have to be made when Sophie comes to stay. She is not immediately enamoured with the idea of sharing her privacy with what she regards as an active nocturnal lizard dancing around her walls and ceiling at night munching and devouring any spiders, flies or other bugs that may have strayed in, thereby making themselves available for dinner. Apart from anything else, geckos do tend to give a small croak in times of exultation, a considered impediment to one's descent into dreamless slumber. She is also initially unenthusiastic about the occasional little reminders he leaves stuck to the wall. Life is not quite like this in London. But she soon comes round to the idea.

The gecko in the machine

This week we have new guests John and Gillian who come from our neck of the woods in the UK. Gillian arrives off the plane looking crisp, cool and dressed for the climate. John is wearing a thick tweed sports jacket, green wool jumper with heavy dark green trousers and a pair of brown leather brogues. He is limping and carrying a stick which does not bode well for sight-seeing or boating. He is hot and bothered and very English with it. Eventually we persuade him to remove his jacket and jumper and he calms down a bit. The following day Gillian spirits him off to George Town for a visit to "Sandpiper" the gifts and clothes shop run by our neighbour Diane. They return triumphant with John resplendent in a short sleeve open necked royal blue shirt with a turquoise turtle motif printed on it. He now looks cool as well. This is judged a great success by us all and, basking in this glow of acclamation, even John seems half convinced. Unfortunately this sartorial progress is somewhat undone several days later when another Brit island friend, Quentin, on introduction to John, enquires "Where on Earth did you get that ghastly shirt?" We do our best to repair John's battered ego and all (including Quentin's wife) round on Quentin pouring justified abuse upon his head. It has to be said that some of Quentin's apparel is questionable; a particularly disreputable pair of seedy old threadbare green shorts come to mind.

During the course of their stay we note a small landmark in life's pattern. John has never learnt to swim and, indeed, is relatively unenthusiastic about water after a sad and devastating event in his childhood. However, in the warm, turquoise, shallow water at Stocking Island he determines to 'have a go'. After advice, encouragement and several attempts he succeeds in swimming a couple of strokes. In the circumstances, it is a heartwarming, brave thing that he has done.

Tonight we are being taken out by our guests of ten days to the Four Seasons hotel's "Sea Breeze" restaurant for drinks and dinner, all of which is expensive and good. The restaurant looks faintly like a converted Oxfordshire barn with a high ceiling and massive roof beams and joists although the illusion is fleeting as they have all been painted white. The tiled floors and ceiling combine acoustically to provide a disconcertingly 'swimming pool' noise; a sort of wet, hollow susurration. Starters of scallops on seared mushrooms are delicious. Certainly my pud, a chocolate confection, is a triumph—a vast heavy chocolate mousse ice cream in a dark chocolate basket with a little jug of fresh raspberry sauce. Truly, death by chocolate! We are served by a rather arrogant little Bahamian waitress. When the bill is presented the cabernet sauvignon proves to have been even more expensive than envisioned by our host but, less acceptably, a rogue bottle of merlot has insinuated itself onto the "check". The waitress announces, gracelessly without pausing for breathe or apology, that her hand must have slipped on the till. A revised bill is substituted and the tip forfeited. We leave contentedly full but mildly irritated by our suspect treatment.

CHAPTER 15

We live in a Wallace and Gromit world. Never mind the "wrong trousers" the water has been off for three days so we ring the local supermarket to confirm that they are off too. "Oh yes de water is off—we have no water—where has all de water gone?" Oh Gromiiiiiit! We thank them politely and ring off having no adequate response to console them with. During the night it has the effect of making the plumbing sound like a dying swan "phew, phew, phew" it goes. L thinks that this may destroy the drains. I think it was this way from the start and we have realised that we shall have to issue bathroom admin rules to our guests as the plumbing is decidedly Greek in some respects.

oooooooo0oooooooo

When daughter Sophie comes to stay at Easter we discover belatedly that her shower seems to be completely unconnected to the drains and the water pours unimpeded in a jolly cascade into the new storeroom below splattering straight onto L's pride and joy, her vastly expensive imported Hayter cylinder lawn mower. ("We must have stripes!") We later find that others seem to have similar plumbing stories. Eventually our Bahamian occasional handyman Paul appears and executes some wondrously Heath Robinson repairs to the exposed drains under the house with what looks like axle grease and smells worse—our elevated position not only gives us a better view but also has the advantage of laying all the plumbing bare for inspection and correction—just as well. The lawn mower is restored to its former state of dignified repose and the large, dark green land crab that has been residing in the grass box is able to return to its home.

ooooooooOooooooooo

We have just heard that our new supermarket manager, owner designate, having given the store a dose of much needed modernisation, has been given the order of the boot and is leaving. If true, this is bad news—there has been no discernable smell of vermin in the supermarket for some months and goodies such as Greek black olives, good cheeses and Ardennes pates were beginning to appear on the shelves. Apparently, Phil the Shelves (for it is he) and his wife "Houseboat Jacqui"(she came to manage the holiday houseboats business) will leave in a fortnight sans job, sans house, sans car just before Christmas having sold up everything in the States to invest in this new adventure. It will probably take four months for the store to sink back into its old lethargic ways—how sad. Since then, we hear mutterings that all was not as it appeared on the surface—there are always two sides to a story, and it must be said he was a chum of our notorious sleeping policeman who had to leave the island in a hurry. R.I.P.

Whatever else the supermarkets are, or are not, they are an essential part of the social fabric of the island. Recently, I overheard a classic conversation between a local and an expat-

Expat: "Is it a Bank Holiday, tomorrow?"
Local: "No, it Labour Day, man"
Expat: "You sure it's not a bank holiday?"

Local: "No! It Labour Day!"
Expat: (deferentially) "But are the banks closed?"
Local: "Yeah, 'course, man!"

And shopping is definitely a social event. Because the four little supermarkets stock differing ranges one quite frequently has to visit all four to complete one's list—which is a wish list not a shopping list. Hence, there is a fair chance of meeting a good proportion of one's friends and associates whilst out and catching up on the latest island gossip. A round trip of all four involving social interaction to a moderate degree can take several hours. For an expert practitioner it can take a half day. Throw in a side swipe to the bank and the telephone company and great chunks of the week can be absorbed and search parties activated.

Buying wine on the island is not a task to be taken lightly, either. Similar to many of the soft drink tins sold locally which are often up to six months past their use by date, wine, which is expensive by any standards, frequently leads one to the conclusion that it has been resting on the dockside somewhere quiet, frying in the sun, because it tastes as though a fish has been hung in it. Caution is recommended when dining out for in a number of establishments on the island lurks a pernicious red wine which the locals offer up enthusiastically and pronounce chateau parroh (emphasis on the second syllable). In fact, it is spelt and I pronounce it "parrot". It tastes as the name would indicate it should.

But the place to find the male of the species is Darvilles, a cavernous crinkly tin warehouse full of hardware from light bulbs to lawn mowers and tools to timber. It is a place to go and meet people whilst browsing in a leisurely way watched over at the entrance/exit by the mountainous Darville "boys". As is so often the case with these sorts of places one stops to marvel at the things in here that are essential that one never realised one needed and things that, intriguingly, perform services one didn't know existed. It is reassuring in these days of inflation and ever higher prices to find that Darvilles' older stock remains at its original value regardless of newer stock arriving on the shelves. So there are occasionally pleasant 'bargains' to be had amongst the tempting stacks of 'objets trouvés'.

CHAPTER 16

We go to St Francis restaurant on adjacent Stocking Island for supper, ringing them and ordering their ferry to collect us from the dock at George Town to cross Queen Elizabeth Harbour. The tables are set out on their stilted-up verandah above their jetty on the side of the little bay and we watch the Sun set in a large scarlet ball through purple clouds on the horizon and then enjoy the magical lights of all the moored yachts and George Town across the water. Passing through the bar I have a seminal moment. A couple are seated on bar stools and the woman has a parrot on her shoulder. I am inspired with a flash of unexpected recognition. I interrupt them: "Excuse me, isn't that an African Grey?" is greeted by an astonished pause and surprised confirmation, "It certainly is!" responds the woman. I say conspiratorially "I once tried to befriend one of those and it damn near took my thumb off!" I am euphoric with this recognition which is only slightly dimmed when I can't find the light in the bathroom and have to return for instructions from a mildly weary barman. The parrot, meanwhile, is showing some ability at cabaret. To attract attention he starts "Flip's a parrot, Flip's a parrot" followed smartly by "Those are nice titties, how much did they cost?"

ooooooooOoooooooo

After a hard day in the Tropics one looks forward to a good rum punch and supper.

This evening the microwave has incinerated a "baked" potato. This is the second time that this has been achieved. The smell is unique and pervasive. If I throw this onto the drive L is sure to complain that the neighbours will be unimpressed. However, the situation is retrieved when L throws it there. In the melee the dog discovers a very large and fearful land crab hiding behind a bougainvillea pot close by. Will the crab eat the potato after we have turned the lights out and left it in peace? Not likely—on rising the following morning we find that the potato is still lying untouched in mute testimony to our microwaving skills. And the land crab has left the field of battle, presumably to find better pickings elsewhere.

oooooooo0oooooooo

L has been playing tennis and is giving the island's vet, Howard and his wife Terri a lift back. It should be said unreservedly that Howard and Terri are both icons of cool but, as the car seems a bit steamy with the heat she decides to open the window. By and by, a very grubby diesel lorry appears coming in the other direction belching fumes, necessitating a swift window close. Howard, unsatisfied, turns on the air conditioning from which a grinding, groaning, being-strangled sort of noise erupts and the interior becomes palpably malodorous. "Ha, ha you've a mouse in there," he chortles, ingenuously amused by his own humour. By the time home is reached squadrons of bluebottles are dive bombing the car to get in, as hard as the suffocating passengers are trying to get out. We consider that maybe the a/c has desiccated a rat. L now expresses concern that, if left unattended, there is a distinct possibility that colonies of maggots will breed swiftly so that the next time the a/c is inadvertently switched on all occupants will be sprayed by a fine diaspora of diced maggot as it is flung out through the air-vent louvres.

We decide that the solution is to take the car to the garage for some 'remedial' work to the a/c and explain our theory to a disbelieving garage man. On returning to collect it Andrew, the proprietor says, "It took me 2 hours with the doors open before I could get near it! That wasn't a mouse; it wasn't even just any ordinary rat—that was a whopper, man! He well chewed up in the a/c!"

Later, as L is leaving the island for a week, she presents me with a matched pair of lavatory "scent" aerosols and parting instructions to "fix the car smell" by the time she returns.

CHAPTER 17

It is 6pm and I am showering prior to changing and going with L to the Peace and Plenty hotel in George Town on the little main street where all gather for fun and riotous assembly of a Friday evening. In the midst of the plashing streams of running water I am assaulted by an ear-splitting rendition of 'Private dancer." It is so loud that I am convinced that L has taken leave of her senses and placed a ghetto blaster on the verandah outside the bathroom, presumably to accelerate my departure from the shower, which is achieved, instantaneously. Soggy and slippery investigation proves this not to be the case and I locate the source as the political "Free National Movement" (FNM) party speaker truck driving past, advertising a rally nearby later this evening, for a general election is in the offing. Here in the Bahamas, charmingly, one is not bludgeoned with political dogma but with pop and calypso music. The view seems to be that the party who plays the loudest wins. The music includes such favourites as "Mama don' like no rake and scrape in hyar" (rake and scrape being a form of primitive calypso played with hand saws, screw drivers and other "instruments" to hand) and the aforementioned "Private dancer". A number of the local songs deal quite frankly with local issues—"Woe is me, shame and scandal in de family" is a no nonsense airing of the problems of local inter-breeding and births outside marriage—most everyone on Exuma is quite loosely, and I use the word advisedly, related to everyone else. My personal favourite is a little number titled "Who put de pepper in de Vaseline".

Friday evening cocktails at the Peace and Plenty are an entirely painless affair lubricated at the 'inside bar' by barman Glenn's anaeshetishing (sic) measures. However, dialogue becomes difficult when the decibel level rises to the inaudible. On this particular night we are standing out on the bar terrace facing Queen Elizabeth's Harbour in a warm and gentle breeze. An enormous orange and heavily overripe moon totters above the horizon and casts a path of shimmering fire across the sea. We are moved to call friends from the bar to witness such a stunning example of nature's beauty.

It is serendipitous to note that, apart from Glenn's profession as barman with his other hat on, he is also the island's paramedic ambulance driver. So if an emergency occurs he is likely to flee the bar for the government clinic down the road and fire up the island ambulance, leaving the bar in the hands of anyone, or on 'honesty'. This vehicle needs more of Glenn's paramedic attention than most of his patients. The juice sapped from the batteries to operate the flashing lights and siren is almost enough to stall the bronchial engine. And as there are no painkillers or other drugs kept on board because the locals pinch them it is advisable to have spent some time receiving Glenn's barman's ministrations before calling on his ambulance abilities.

After cocktails at the "P and P" for an hour or two, and this is quite enough given the super-generous portions served up by the bar, it is time to move on to the Exuma Fish Fry. As we pass through reception the beautiful black girl behind the desk advises us that there is a dance here on the morrow. Audley Dames and the Sweet Love Band will be playing and there is a cover charge of $5. "It start at ten o' clock, man."

"Heavens, that's late!"

"No man, de natives get restless at ten!" she beams.

A collection of permanent shacks painted rasta colours a mile out of town on the beach front, the Fish Fry serves up Bahamian cooking most nights with gusto and a lot of loud music and still more refreshments for those with the stamina. Because it is a "no bottle zone" the booze is served up in plastic cups which effectively stops the locals from beating each other over the head with the empty bottles later in the evening, as things become more lively. It is noteworthy that, unlike certain locations in the UK, the combatants do not break the bottles before joining battle. Now its time to eat and orders are placed over a small let-down counter at the side of the shack whilst we go and bag seats on one of the long twelve seater picnic benches on the deck by the beach bar. Food comes in takeaway format in a Styrofoam "shell" and flip-top lid with a plastic knife and fork. The blackboard menu lists BBQ chicken, ribs, souse (meat boiled in brine—just like old fashioned school food, disgusting), breaded shrimps (these are vast and done in batter—spectacular and delicious) or conch on offer tonight. For the uninitiated, conch (pronounced conk) is a large snail-like mollusc with a beautiful shell. Cinematically speaking they are best remembered when, alluringly, two conch shells emerged from the sea with Ursula Andress stealing the scene in the James Bond movie "Dr No" to the strains of "Underneath de mango tree . . ." "sung" by Miss Andress and Sean Connery. Conch are usually cooked in batter and taste like squids rings. Served up with coleslaw, peas and rice, or French fries (chips to us) some of the island staples, these combinations send the health rev counter for fat and cholesterol to the red line so we tend to swap them for lettuce and tomato. All is consumed and washed down with immense good fellowship. By 9.30 we are wending our way homeward to bed in a happy haze. Tomorrow one may reasonably expect to be Saturday.

Shore to shoe—a mature conch shell beside a
pair of size 7 flipflops

CHAPTER 18

My favourite place to go for a long, laid-back lunch is "Santana's" a sleepy, octagonal beach bar and grill painted in Rastafarian colours of bright yellow, green, red, ochre and blue, named after the daughter of the owners. It sits between the end of the Queen's Highway (single lane, potholed in each direction) at the southern tip of Little Exuma, and the beach. There is no through traffic because there is nowhere to go. The sun always seems to shine and the heat fairly bounces off the tarmac. All one's fellow diners sit round the counters facing the turquoise sea and its improbably white surf with the cooking and booze in the middle making for such an amiable atmosphere of good fellowship that it is pretty much impossible not to join in the general conversations.

Today, we are taking our son Ben and daughter-in-law Melissa who are holidaying with us, to Santana's for lunch. Dee, who runs it with her husband Edgar, is a big girl with a wonderful, broad smile and laugh to match and a warm welcome for everyone; Edgar on the other hand who does the fishing for the grill is just sinew and bone, skin blackened by action of the sun's rays and the sea. Dee's drink measures are in proportion to her personality and ferocious. On this occasion I have a G and T which comes in a pint, da-glo pink tinted plastic cup while we are ordering and the others have Kalik beers and various rum cocktails. I order a cracked conch; tenderised and cooked in batter, it chews like large pieces of calamari and comes with copious coleslaw, garlic fried onions and sweetcorn. L will have shrimps: these are a magnificent, three to four inches across done in batter. The youngsters will have lobster, which we Brits call crayfish. By the time the food arrives my drink is nearly finished with a little help from my friends, principally L. I am in mellow mood and turn to my son to ask him if he would like to try some of my food. I mean to say "Would you like a mouthful of my cracked conch" unfortunately my G and T and the Reverend Spooner take a hand and what I actually come out with is a spoonerism of spectacularly lewd proportions which I leave to your imagination. There is a short pause as people consider whether they have misheard and then we are incapacitated with laughter: my daughter in law is reduced to making mewing noises between tears. Fortunately the other diners are far enough away not to have heard my faux pas and so some well-battered dignity is retained. After everyone is sated we move off up-island to the wide coral sand crescent that is Tropic of Cancer beach. It is time to fall into its warm, clear, blue waters to ease off some lunch and catch some sunshine whilst admiring the two Robinson Crusoe islands which provide it with shelter from the ocean before heading back to change for the evening.

oooooooo0oooooooo

The whole island has been intrigued for some time about the filming of "Pirates of the Caribbean" some of which took place on Little Exuma, which is attached to the southern tip of Great Exuma by the long, low "Ferry" bridge that is well past its sell by date. All the stars were present, in particular, Johnny Depp and Orlando Bloom, who caused a major sensation and were photographed numerously with Dee at Santana's for posterity. A well-worn photograph album containing the appropriate evidence is available for perusal at the merest hint to Dee.

As I am emerging from the boat yard in the Victoria Pond in George Town I pass a silver saloon car and one of the island's rogues, the villainous giant Neville, is revealed within. "What are you doing in that?" I ask, because he usually drives a truck inscribed "I love kayaking". He explains in detail, whereupon L follows out and repeats the same question verbatim. Neville stares at her and after a pause, says, "You two are like parrots—yes that's what you are, parrots". I lay a reassuring hand on his vast forearm and respond cheerfully, "Yes, Neville, we're parrots of the Caribbean!"

oooooooo0oooooooo

Sunday in the Bahamas is taken fairly seriously. The Exumans, by and large, are quite religious and pack the churches of all denominations, including a surprising quantity of minority cults and breakaway sects, in significant numbers. Those attending are almost unrecognisable from their day to day persona. The men wear dark suits and brilliant white shirts with exuberant ties, while the womenfolk look stunning: imagine a crowd at Ascot in its pomp some years ago and this gives some impression of the congregations: the very best shoes, nylons and dresses are worn with flamboyant hats and hand-bags more akin to a wedding than a mere Sunday. The whole creates an enormous air of joyous festivity stimulated by the gospel singing. But here a note of caution, services can go on for as long as two and a half hours.

The contrast with the rest of the week and particularly Friday and Saturday nights could not be more striking. It has to be said that, like religion, the people take their pleasure and their sex lives seriously, as well. Many married couples are in their second or more relationship so that the communities up and down the island are populated by their "in" and "out" children, that is to say, those born in and out of wedlock. Consequently, it is always unwise in a moment of frustration with a local tradesman (and there are plenty of these!) to mutter about him in someone else's hearing; invariably they will be related.

ooooooooOooooooooo

We have just popped back to the UK and L has remained there until the end of the week to complete various tedious but necessary admin functions. So now I am a "holiday bachelor:"—principal rôle, emptying the dog. The thing about bachelorhood is that, apart from all the deteriorating relics of mysterious and congealing, furry food items congesting the fridge, one becomes very clear about all the jobs that need doing around the place. In a mere fortnight a reasonably well ordered garden has become a tropical jungle: weeds have appeared—boy, have they appeared! Large bushes have sprouted in previously barren ground where we usually park the cars and these have mature creepers growing through them already. Massive "Railroad Vines" (Ipomoea pes-caprae also called Beach morning Glory, a member of the convolvulus family) snake across the flower beds and up any trees available. Jack and the Beanstalk isn't a fairytale—it happens and I'm in it! As all the Haitians (and the illegal French Canadians etc, etc,) have been run off the island by the immigration stormtroopers, there is nobody to help retrain this vegetable circus so its roll up the sleeves time. One intriguing surprise is that L's "extinct" basil has seeded profusely and we now have a basil forest. This is not quite where we wanted it but then natural forests seldom are. Nevertheless, (the royal) we will be very pleased at how much we've got when she returns. I am not entirely sure what one does with a very large quantity of basil; I suppose its very good for you—no doubt the French would apply it to some obscure part of the anatomy. Still, better that a suppository.

oooooooo0ooooooooo

We have been subjected to our first Tropical Storm, not just any old storm but one that comes within the meteorological definition of winds up to 73 mph with rain to match. It is a real Shakespeare's "Tempest". As we watch, mesmerised from the house this enormous squall moves with daunting speed across the ocean towards us; a dark, bruise blue-grey blanket behind which, from a distance, all appears to be obliterated, gobbling up the sea as it comes. As an earnest of nature's raw power it provides an awe-inspiring example. It is accompanied by a howling wind which induces what I call "running out the guns"—where the plastic chairs on our verandah are all thrust over and hurtle pell-mell rumbling down the deck to form a motley heap at the downwind end. The rain is a constant deluge as though the bath taps of heaven have been turned full on and the water cascades off the roof in sheeting torrents. (It's not the done thing to have gutters in the Bahamas). Then our ears are riven with a thunderous percussion as lightning slits the clouds and shows us the very antithesis of the sunny warm place we know—a hellish view of a grey waterscape. Now we realise why many houses don't bother with gutters and downcomers. In these circumstances they are an irrelevance.

Down goes the internet so we decide swiftly to unplug all the electricals and turn off all the fuses at the box to await the inevitable power cut. Unusually, this doesn't happen on this occasion. We have surge protectors on our computer equipment and a master unit covering the whole house by way of belt and braces. This is on advice that when the local electricity powers up after what the locals call an "outage" (more of an outrage in my view) they are unable to control it and tend to fry all unwary electrical equipment. Replacement from the States is the solution but this is an extremely expensive option given the costs of shipping and eye-watering customs duty rates.

After the storm, which subsequently becomes a hurricane as it moves off up the American coast, we emerge to assess the situation. Our section of the island is cut off from George Town and the airport to the north. The airport is also cut off from the hotel up island. Nevertheless, the airlines resume service so quantities of weary travellers arrive here with no prospect of transport and no hotel at the airport. Eventually they are brought out by lorry and flat-bed truck as no taxis or cars can get through on the Queen's Highway because the floods are too deep for them. L goes to a "drop off point" to give some friends a lift to their house and "everyone is there". In the course of this highly social event she engages in conversation with an irate Bahamian while she waits for "her" truck to arrive. "Dey shouldn't be flyin' into de airport," he says, "It's supposed to be shut because dey got no fire engine, so dere's no safety." "How would you know?" enquires L. "Because I'm de fire engine driver!"

oooooooooOoooooooo

This evening we celebrate our first year in the Bahamas. With ten chums we are going again to St Francis restaurant on Stocking Island taking their ferry, the good ship Ruby 11, for the nine minute trip. In about a month, on or after the Americans celebrate Thanksgiving the seven mile stretch of sheltered water known as the Harbour will fill up with some 300 yachts as the "boaters" return for the winter season which lasts until April the following spring. Our young 18 year old skipper whisks us out from the dock for one of the first night-time trips now that the 'daylight saving' is in operation and the hour has gone back. (Much argument with L as to which way the clocks go until a helpful Canadian friend announces, "Springs forward, Falls back" and I now have a mantra to remember it by). As we progress across the harbour in the dark, admiring the Stocking Island and yacht lights reflecting on the water the skipper comes out of the cabin to chat to us. After some time it becomes apparent that we are on auto-pilot; nobody is on watch. One of our number, a Fastnet race veteran, gives the poor youngster a sound dressing down on the possibility of broken down dinghies without lights, together with flotsam and jetsam lying on the surface in the dark. The skipper retreats, chastened, to the helm. I feel sorry for him—after all we are all young, gregarious and enthusiastic once. But our veteran is, of course, absolutely right and very soon, in addition to the hazards already mentioned, will be added the anchor chains plus other ill-lit equipment of the 300 odd moored yacht armada waiting to snare the unsuspecting.

Our meal is great fun and in the drowsy heat of the tropical night we are well fuelled. Fortunately, we order six plates of conch fritters as a starter to stave off starvation while the main courses are prepared at a snails pace, much like most things at this latitude. Our erstwhile skipper has now metamorphosed into his other persona, that of our waiter who is as attentive and courteous as he was on the boat. The fritters are excellent, batter good and crispy with plenty of succulent conch flesh inside to guzzle into. They come with a Thousand Islands dressing as an optional dip. We are informed by a friend that the dressing originated in Canada on the Great Lakes where the eponymous islands can be found. Our main courses are split between calamari and steak Béarnaise with French fries or salads depending on the waistlines of the diners. Our tables, three pulled end to end, are outside on the restaurant verandah and we look back towards George Town, lit up on the black water as the sky above is a patchwork quilt of stars hung with a hammock tropical moon.

On the return journey, conversation is muted as we are lulled by the warm breeze and the gentle swell of the ocean while the ferry ploughs its way stolidly back towards the dock, leaving a trail of glittering phosphorescence behind us.

CHAPTER 19

I am looking forward to Christmas for it is mid-December. I don't know how it is in other countries but it is, oh joy! very "quick" here, by which I mean there is no retail build up from September the way there is in the UK, which always seems fairly obscene. The first hint of festivity on the island occurred when the local supermarkets started pumping out carols across their PA systems about two weeks ago, followed by the appearance of some small and very coy displays of lights, tinsel, wrapping paper etc in the least used corners of the shops. Amazingly, one can buy mincemeat but not decent sausages or sausagemeat. Stuffing has the consistency of small lumps of damp cardboard and is, consequently, inedible except to ravenous cockroaches. Visiting a nearby hostelry for drinks we come across a life-size effigy of Santa Claus and are intrigued to discover that Santa is, of course, black at least in the Tropics! This comes as a surprise to those of us who have spent their formative years in the sheltered bosom of Britain. Most importantly, Christmas is quiet, warm and sunny!

On the Queen's Highway to the North of us lies the CNK liquor store and "Smitty's," one of the little local supermarkets. Upon its roof teeters a magnificent inflatable Santa who is tethered by a stout rope around his feet to restrain him from flight in the unseasonable wind. He jigs and sways, lolling majestically with one hand raised in a permanent wave and a beatific alcoholic smile on his face, undoubtedly a liquor store customer with excess Christmas cheer consumed; it is just as well he cannot speak. A colleague of his in the Peace and Plenty hotel sings "Happy Christmas Baby" when one passes him. Elvis is alive and well and lives here in Exuma and don' anyone tell you different—baby! "Thang you verrr much."

ooooooooOoooooooo

It being the season of good cheer, L has been out and bought copious strings of fairy lights to beautify the garden. And very pretty they look from the verandah, twinkling and swaying in the trees on the breeze. They are so awesomely cheap as to be virtually disposable and are made in China. Unfortunately, the inscrutable Chinee has seen fit to insert some fiendishly heathen system into them which makes them flash or, to be more accurate, half the length of one of the strings flashes stroboscopically whilst the rest maintain a tranquil, steady glow. Apparently, this is quite unsatisfactory. It must be all or nothing and entreaties along the lines of "but what about a bit of contrast" fall on deaf ears. L wants me (why me?) to return them to the shop and say that they are faulty. I am resisting this on the grounds that, firstly I didn't buy them and, more likely for sure, the shop assistant will look pityingly at me and say condescendingly "You <u>have</u> pressed the ying tong foo button?" thinking all the while "Who is this incompetent buffoon?", thus exposing again how ignorant I am about these embarrassing simplicities of life.

Addendum, L returns from the shop and the "button" turns out to be a clear bulb—who's just a pretty face, then! However, the plot thickens when two of the sets turn out not to have a clear bulb, but a comprehensive search identifies a rogue coloured bulb with a flasher switch in it. Its life is brutish and short. Equilibrium is restored to our tranquil Christmas setting—the lights have achieved steady state.

This shopping mission has also produced a novel confusion. L has been charged with making and supplying a trifle for eleven souls for Christmas dinner with friends. Having looked unsuccessfully round the shelves she asks at the check-out (till) "Do you have any Birds Powdered Custard?" A blank look is followed by a deep Bahamian scowl of disbelief "Powdered custard for BIRDS?!" Explanation and enlightenment follows.

I have had a similar experience the other day. We and CNK Liquor had run out of gin. But I knew that our friends the Johnsons were going up island because the store there had a sale running so I rang and got the manageress. "Charmaine, do you have Simon Johnson in the store at the moment?" "I'm sorry sir, we don't carry that brand."

ooooooooOooooooooo

As Sophie is arriving for a week over the Christmas hols I have been deputed to obtain information about diving; she acquired her PADI certificate in the wintry, murky, February waters off Beadnell in Northumberland. I present myself at the Exuma Starfish adventure Centre office just down the road; beside the office is a large sign inscribed "Exuma Dive". A very polite chap in the office says that Starfish don't do diving and that the dive office is on the other side of George Town at the February Point resort. I leave, confused and ignorant with a fistful of leaflets one of which, on subsequent inspection clearly states that the Exuma Dive office is beside Starfish—whence I have just come.

ooooooooOooooooooo

On the outskirts of George Town lies Sam's Dock, a series of jetties supported on fat telegraph poles with fresh water and fuel for large yachts and motor cruisers. Moored here is the "Emerald Lady" a fine 46 foot catamaran which does day cruises up and down Queen Elizabeth Harbour. It being the Christmas hols we have taken our little 18 foot boat and motored across the Harbour to a deserted beach on Stocking Island, the long protective reef opposite Great Exuma. We make camp; parasol for the dog; tarpaulin and towels for us between the high and low tide mark and stake out for some sunbathing, L, daughter and me, that is. After some time I look up to check that the boat's anchor is not dragging in the sand bottom and see the Emerald Lady all sails aloft heading straight for us in our little bay. I alert the girls who watch proceedings with interest. About 50 feet offshore she executes a perfect gybe and sails off in the other direction. I point out that we are obviously now on the Lady's itinerary and are, consequently, tourist icons.

CHAPTER 20

After a week's holiday with us, our daughter returned to the UK yesterday: we decide it would be fun to link up with friends Howard and Terry and walk our various dogs, all of whom are great chums. Howard suggests that we all go in their boat and Terry promises that she will stop their poodle Nicole from causing mayhem by flirting too outrageously with Habu. We motor across Queen Elizabeth Harbour to Stocking Island; there is a brisk wind with plenty of chop and whitecaps, even so, Howard's boat is a well designed twin-vee (catamaran type hull) powered by two large outboard motors and the trip is dry.

We moor on the jetty in Hamburger Bay, so called because the Peace and Plenty hotel in George Town on Exuma boasts a shack outpost here which sells junk food lunches, beer and cans of soft drinks. We all have conch burgers which are excellent and quite spicy with the local Bahamas brew "Kalik" drunk direct from the bottle in the traditional manner.

After lunch we vote to amble over Stocking and walk along the beach on the Atlantic side. It is still a lovely warm sunny day and five foot waves crash impressively on the beach. The sea, too, is warm and Howard decides that as he can see a sandy stretch in the water, he will go in for a swim, which he does. Several minutes later I follow but encounter coral and rock which makes for unsteady footing and after being shoved about in thigh high water, decide to come out. Meanwhile Howard has swum out almost beyond the breakers to where the waves are predominantly blue water and seems to be enjoying himself. He waves his arm in an encouraging fashion and shouts something we cannot hear so Terry decides she will go out too. Once they are both out there I think that riding the waves, as they are, may be fun and follow. Having taken a pounding to arrive out with them I realise that, contrary to my initial assessment of having fun, they are both in big trouble—and so am I. (We also discover afterwards that Terry has realised that Howard is, in fact, waving goodbye and has entered the water because she cannot bear to be without him). A vicious rip tide is operating which will not allow us to swim back to the beach, a tantalising 25 yards away. We waste considerable energy trying to fight the current to no avail whilst my wife sits placidly with the dogs watching us, totally unaware that a life-threatening situation is unfolding before her. Any attempts at waving and shouting are lost in the noise of the breakers but no one has surplus energy for this, in any event. At last Howard, who has lived here for some years yells that we must swim north, parallel to the beach so that we can cross the currents further up. We all attempt this with tortuous lack of progress. However, in the end, I see that Howard and Terry have made it to the beach but do not realise that Howard is immobile with fatigue and Terry is in a state of horror watching my impending demise.

Meanwhile, my predicament appears not to have improved. I am swimming/floating on my back and becoming very tired having spent longer than the others trying to swim a direct line to Linda and the dogs so close on the beach. Frequently I can see nothing but sky—no land visible, at all. As each huge wave rolls towards me I hope that it will stay blue: I know I will ride over these and can continue swimming. When a breaker appears I must take a beep breath, hold my nose and close my eyes as the white frothing wall sweeps over, engulfing me and forcing me to regroup before starting to swim again. Dauntingly, three out of every four waves are breakers. A depressing feature of the whole episode has been periodically finding bottom with my feet only to realise that, as I am being swept off it by another breaker, it is just another rock outcrop in the midst of much deeper water. Another consideration is that these outcrops are full of potholes and catching a foot could mean a broken limb at best, and at worst . . . .

As soon as the others have alerted her to the apparent danger Linda has run for help with Habu, who would have forged into the sea on a rescue mission and surely drowned, if left to his own devices. I am becoming exhausted with the buffeting breakers and, while floating immobile to rest for a short time, offer up a small prayer. Then the next wave covers me and fills my mouth and nostrils with yet another cascading torrent of saltwater. Soon after, I am so exhausted that I believe I am going to die by drowning within twenty five yards of safety, a conclusion of futility almost too sad to bear. The waves take a short break between pounding me and, in order to rest my aching arms and shoulders, I decide to tread water. As my feet go down, to my amazement, they touch—just—genuine sand for a second before another wave lifts me out of my depth again. But in its aftermath I am planted back on the sand once more. I dig my feet in and push with every surviving ounce of strength towards the beach and begin slowly and painfully making progress towards the shore. After finally collapsing on the waterline I join the other two lying further up the beach—unable to move with fatigue and a stomach bloated with sea water. Roused by Linda, help arrives in the shape of a TV producer who has been filming on the island. Determined on rescue, he brings a long rope, (which, we later discover he knows will almost certainly not be long enough) flippers and bottles of water. Finding that the worst is over, he takes over the resuscitation process making sure we re-hydrate and take on sugar to recover. In the end, all of us, and the dogs, have survived and made an extremely fortunate escape. To come to terms with all this requires several weeks, days and nights of unwelcome mental "playback". I have always regarded the sea with respect but now I am determined not to give it a second chance ever again if I can possibly avoid it.

CHAPTER 21

One has to say that the climate has been generally disappointing this last year—much more cloud, wind and rain than usual, or expected, and less calm, sunny days than hoped for. Still there have been no hurricanes, the weather has been good for gardening and the place looks surprisingly mature all considered. Blooming hibiscus, oleander, allamanda, frangipani and bougainvillea are all a joy. A real surprise has been that some of the coconuts we stuffed into the ground in the spring have produced shoots—our own coconut palms, personally grown! Moreover the grapefruit pip that L planted is now a tree fifteen feet high with vicious defensive thorns and requires regular pruning. No grapefruit yet, though. We have about five varieties of palm in the garden—a fairly restrained collection considering the forty odd species that grow in these parts. L has two lawns (isn't it strange how lawn rhymes with yawn?) which keeps her busy mowing and happy. They are definitely an asset to the garden but, as may be surmised, I have absolutely no ego on this issue! The island becomes even more spectacular as the season moves into May and June when the Royal Poincianas come into bloom. Across the island's length and breadth are quantities of these trees growing wild: frequently reaching 20 feet high they become covered in a scarlet carpet of flowers obscuring their delicate fern-like leaves. There are so many of them that this carpet is clearly visible from the air if one is flying in. When the blossom is finished the seed pods appear hanging, like so many two foot long boomerangs dangling from all the branches. Because they rattle well they are occasionally used elsewhere in the Caribbean by the locals as maracas or "shak-shaks". The seeds themselves are about an inch long coming in a flat banana-shaped brown husk.

A real eye-opener is how fast everything grows here in the Tropics. The summer is the rainy (and hurricane) season and so we take the opportunity to go back to the UK to see family and friends and catch up on some admin. On our return, the garden has become a jungle and in the middle of the path immediately in front of the steps leading to the porch is a tree. This tree was not there when we left and is now ten feet high with a proper tree trunk etcetera. We are nonplussed but decide it just has to go—it is a wild variety and not one worth transplanting. However, a similar story lurks beside it but off the path. A pink Poui which has rich shiny leaves like a rhododendron with beautiful fluted pale pink flowers has seeded itself and this we can and do move to a better place.

Our garden has been a mixture of success and failure: vegetables have disappointed frustratingly given their cost and unreliable availability at the local supermarkets while flowers, shrubs and trees have delighted.

Potatoes, lettuces and other greens could not survive the heat of the Caribbean sun so we gave them up, (but are intending to try them again using grow bags under netting with a "weepy" watering system.) However tomatoes have been a revelation. Spectacular crops have kept on and on coming from a small number of plants grown from seed kindly donated by Cynthia. In fact, at least one meal a day has been, basically, tomatoes for the fruiting period of some three months.

At last, our Persian lime tree, planted as a seedling some time ago has fruited copiously and we are the beneficiaries of the most mouth-watering little green limes for our evening G and Ts, picked fresh straight from the garden to the glass. Sadly, we have had no success trying to propagate Royal Poinciana trees, although we have two lovely wild specimens on the edge of our land which are about fifteen feet high—quite small considering that they can grow to 40ft.

Fortunately, we were bemoaning our propagation shortcomings to a friend and she gave us a couple of compensatory Pride of Barbados seedlings. These waifs were languishing in little plastic flower pots when we put them beside the house and forgot about them. Not for long. Soon came the day when we asked ourselves what the weeds were that were growing up the side of the trellis. To our astonishment the answer was the 'Prides' which had blasted tap roots through the bottoms of the pots and were doing a beanstalk growing fast in all directions with trunks the size of a man's wrist in no time. They seed prolifically, which is immensely satisfying as they are sometimes known as the false Poinciana. However, unlike the Poinciana they flower nearly all year round with a profusion of hallucinatory crimson and orange blossoms which are beautiful (hence the latin name Caesalpina pulcherrima), and make superb flower arrangements. Broadcasting the seeds can have dramatic success, which is just as well because the little seedlings hate being transpanted unless they are tiny.

Night flowering stock was not a success but a surprise substitute is a large local bush which produces a profusion of little white flowers which smell similarly sublime, during the day. Another triumph are the Allamanda which come in both dwarf and full size varieties. These are also known as Yellow Bell, Golden Trumpet or Buttercup Flower, having green rhododendron-type leathery lance like, pointed leaves. Year round they produce large bright yellow flowers.

Our Bougainvillea have survived and prospered although one on an exposed corner of the house was ripped out by a strong wind, recently; it must have been highly focussed because nothing else was touched. 'Bougies' are mostly planted to grow through the trees which provide a supportive frame work, creating an illusion that the host tree is blossoming in hot pinks and purples.

A winter favourite is the Desert Rose, which is a succulent, having scant leathery leaves with eye-catching flowers in a pink and white blush produced in February and March. Pot grown, they respond best when living in dry, cramped conditions to add a blaze of colour to our porch.

ooooooooOooooooooo

There used to be four places on the island where one could get gas (petrol to us), two filling stations in George Town, a pump on the garage forecourt at the north end of the island near Emerald Bay and the "Blessed Full" filling station in between. Unfortunately, despite its religious appeal, the Blessed Full garage is now derelict and being swiftly reclaimed by the jungle, a testament to the enthusiasm of the owners who, presumably in matching the Lord's interests with that of keeping customers' tanks full, sought to achieve this by watering down the fuel with dire results for the vehicles and, ultimately, themselves when the police got wind of it.

One of the island garages rejoices in the name "Cool Runnings" from the eponymous film about the Jamaican 1988 winter Olympics bobsleigh entry; a rather catchy title in a land where marketing is in its infancy. And a missed opportunity is the hardware shop that goes by the name of Grog Pond—what a wonderful name for a liquor store!

ooooooooOooooooooo

Payment of outstanding bills is always a flexible event on Exuma and our veterinarian friend Howard has liberated a small poodle in exchange for unpaid services. In order to train it he bought an electric collar and remote control which issues a shock to the dog's neck. The other day he went into George Town in the car with the dog on the passenger seat. Halting the traffic to chat, as is the norm, he joined in an animated discussion with several others from his driver's window. After some little time, he became aware that while he was conversing enthusiastically the dog had unexpectedly developed a hitherto undiagnosed but frequent facial twitch. After further heated debate he realised that each of his gesticulations was activating the remote in his pocket and the poor dog!

CHAPTER 22

Normally, hurricanes don't bother us much. But every morning during hurricane season we check a magnificent website called 'Stormcarib', just to keep an eye on the brutes. It not only shows where the hurricanes are but does a five day forecast plotting their routes and closest point to you during that period. The season is generically between June first and November thirtieth, although the actual high risk period for Exuma is pretty much during September and October.

However, on this occasion there are two coming up towards the Bahamas. As the first, "Hanna" comes closer people suddenly find they have urgent business to attend to in the States and begin to leave in droves together with all the guests from the hotel at the north end of the island who are compulsorily evacuated. We put up our hurricane shutters on the front door and all the windows and sit in the gloom to await it.

In the event it does a swerve and nothing much happens as it moves slowly off towards Florida. (These things quite often only travel at five to ten miles an hour.) But what does happen is a lot less attractive: its passing reveals hurricane Ike lurking immediately behind in all its malevolent glory.

This beast is now upgraded to category 4—sustained winds of between 131 and 155 miles per hour—and one level below the maximum category 5. We consider what it would do to the island

and our house. Probably, there would be severe damage to most buildings, significant flooding and total loss of water, electricity and telecommunications for a prolonged period, certainly weeks and more than likely, months. Whether the island's only airport would be usable for some time after is a moot point.

Then I decide to check Ike's closest point to us on the website. It will reach land 1 mile from George Town in 48 hours. As we are 2 miles up the coast from George Town that makes its landfall potentially, at best, 3 miles from us and at worst 1 mile! Although we could probably survive the devastation caused by a category 4 direct hit we fear for our German Shepherd Habu and decide to evacuate pronto. This is easier said than done; the last flights on the scheduled aircraft are all full and D-day is on Saturday, 2 days away. Isn't it interesting how crises always erupt on Fridays, during weekends or on Bank Holidays? Concerned, we ring the air charter shipper to the island. Yes they have a six seater twin engine plane flying out on Friday beating the hurricane's arrival—always assuming it can fly in and get out all right.

We throw some stuff in a couple of bags, grab the dog and flee to the airport. It is already raining with dark forbidding clouds massing. There is only one other passenger who mercifully has two Chihuahuas. They look nervous and Habu looks hungry; nevertheless, détente is maintained. The pilot is bald with a protruding stomach and by the time we are in the air he is sweating profusely and is a candidate for a coronary, in my opinion. I wonder idly what would happen if he has one—can our fellow passenger fly this thing—if not, could I? I am not hopeful; I can't remember the phonetic alphabet for call signs even when relaxed—I always want to say "G george" and just know it's something else, so my chances of doing a cliché talk-down as in the films are slim to non existent. But he looks vaguely familiar and suddenly I recognise him.

"He IS the mad, druggy doctor from the film Cannonball Run!" I whisper to L.

"Oh Heavens, so he is," she gasps.

As if in confirmation of this we attempt to engage him in banal conversation as much to assuage our own fears as anything but we get no response. Eventually he begins to receive messages in his earphones, presumably from Fort Lauderdale control tower at our destination

"I can't hear ya," he replies.

"Repeat."

"Whaaat?"

"Repeat"

"I CAN'T HEAR YA!"

It appears that he is aurally challenged, as well.

After bouncing around the sky for some time we see the welcome sight of the Florida coastline ahead. However, above is a humungous, lowering saucer-shaped cloud of black sky like an imagination-defyingly large alien spaceship.

"What is THAT?" we yell: it looks as though hurricane Ike has done a flanker and is waiting for us ahead. Dialogue is achieved.

"That's the hurricane" The pilot bellows.

"Sorry? . . . surely not."

"Yeah, ... it's Hanna."

"Er . . . . So what happens now?" I shout, only mildly falsetto.

"Oh, we just gotta go underneath it!"

Indeed, shortly we begin a shallow dive and commence what seems like a bombing run skimming across the ocean surface towards the airport; I feel like the Dambusters. The runway rears up to meet us and, to be fair, our doctor friend performs an immaculate landing.

We are mopped up by our highly efficient shipper, taken to a car hire company and thence to our hotel. The hotel is dog-friendly and we have booked in advance. On arrival, we approach the reception desk wearily except for Habu, who has very occasional lapses of social etiquette (on his first visit to a pub he leapt onto a table) and, in a proprietary manner marches up to the desk, rises majestically on his hind-legs, plants his fore-paws on the ink blotter and sticks his muzzle in the receptionist's face. This creates a certain frisson but, calming the poor girl, we are able to register. She tells us we have a room on the ground floor "Because that's where most of the dog people like to be". I note a sign beside the lift which says "Do not enter the elevator when flashing" and, having checked surreptitiously that I am decent, settle down for a brief respite in Reception, knowing from experience that until L has screened the room and is satisfied it is pointless to lug the cases along there, not to say extremely unwise to start unpacking. She takes the key and Habu, disappearing meaningfully on the tour of inspection and returns shortly with an enigmatic and impenetrable expression. It seems that the room was at car park level and looked straight onto a parked car. Habu took a dim view of it, gave the place a good, disdainful sniff then smartly lifted his leg and shot a monster pee down the bottom bedpost. We swap for a room on the second floor, above flood level (for Hanna, not Habu) and with a nice view of the adjacent lake, ("No swimming, possibility of fresh water crocodiles").

After a novel week in Fort Lauderdale, (the hotel was good but had no restaurant, OK—ish and no bar, WHAT!?), the hurricanes have passed and it is time to return to Exuma. The shippers will take Habu as freight but not us as passengers, so we fly scheduled with Continental. Back at George Town airport we await his return nervously. The shipper swears that their plane left on schedule and should be here any time. At last, half an hour late, a speck appears, grows and lands. Half way down the runway it collapses onto the tarmac before our horrified eyes. The undercarriage has been causing problems resulting in the delay, and has just given up the ghost altogether. On board, apart from Habu, is a large box of Iguanas which are being returned to the cays after a 'scientific study' vacation. Both are unloaded onto the tarmac into the searing heat of the early afternoon and the crystal clear skies left by the hurricane's wake, Habu in his plastic travel cage.

We remonstrate with Customs and Security, being passed from one to the other. In the end L throws a 'wobbler' of category four proportions which alarms the officials enough for us to be escorted up the apron to collect him. To say that he is pleased to see us would be a masterly understatement but the poor dog has to dance all the way back to the terminal building because the tarmac is so hot it is burning his feet. On the way home we stop at the beach and he makes a dead run for the sea plodging in and out of the waves with evident glee. Who says dogs can't smile?

ooooooooOoooooooo

In a moment of levity I have let slip that I am writing an occasional diary. Our friends Simon and Cynthia are intrigued to know whether they are in it. As the answer is yes and Simon is in one of his 'Tiggerish' moods I ask him what name he would prefer to be known by, in case I have to use pseudonyms. He asks if his brother-in-law Norman is also to feature. This is a yes, too. I suggest that nothing less than a knighthood would be appropriate in the circumstances so he settles for "Sir Simon de Goombay" (the name of their house), insisting on "serf Norman" for his brother-in-law.

During a subsequent meal Simon is reminded of his status as Sir Simon de Goombay, Knight of the Realm. It is pointed out that, in the circumstances, he needs a coat of arms. After some confusion, it is explained to him that this is a heraldic design unique to himself and not an article of clothing. Much merriment is then derived from the assembled guests' views as to what heraldic devices should be illustrated, the least of which include balls and a wine bottle couchant, the rest being quite unprintable.

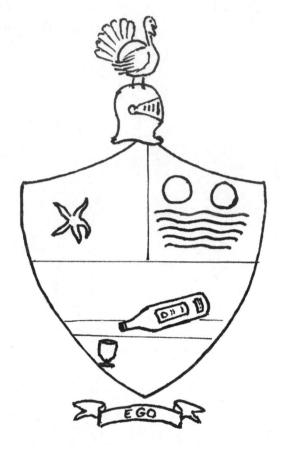

The de Goombay coat of arms:

Crest: A turkey perched, wattled of gules

Shield: A starfish proper embowed, azure three bezants or,
argent a wine bouget couchant

CHAPTER 23

We meet our new neighbours Steven and Miriam and ask them in for a drink. He is dark and satanic and it transpires that he is something in re-insurance with Lloyds underwriters, we think, and she is tall, blonde and Brazilian. They have owned a house on the island before and are returning and building again after an absence of some years, unable to stay away. Their project manager's partner has offered them landscaping services in addition to supervising their house-build, sending them photographs from his portfolio of work. Our neighbour is insulted and incensed because in front of the most favoured shot is, unmistakably, a large and florid garden gnome.

As it turns out, this is an ominous portent of things to come. As the build commences it becomes clear that the designated builder has very little experience of house construction. This is compounded by a number of swift changes by various enthusiasts to the plans and house location. In due course a back hoe (JCB is the English equivalent) arrives on site driven by a large and thunderous Bahamian. Under his auspices the house foundations commence a square dance around the site. When the music stops the house is a good twelve feet nearer the water's edge and a patio has been contrived which, in its folly, lies absolutely on the high tide line. This appears to have been built by a man with a bad squint or a limp, or possibly both. Its outer retaining wall, which borders the beach itself, has been built with breeze blocks; no levelling instrument of any kind has been used, so far as one can tell. The bottom course of blocks starts at a point and lurches crazily downwards arriving at the other end of the patio façade some six inches lower. All subsequent courses follow this dubious example. This forms an interesting architectural contrast with the house behind which has, in fact, been appropriately built on a horizontal axis. The result is unique. The body of the patio has been filled with builders' rubble, lunchtime refuse and beach sand together with the occasional small tree trunk uprooted during the site clearance.

One morning during this spell a uniquely disgusting smell pervades the house. Emerging onto the verandah I see that the Bahamian labourers on the site have lit a bonfire from which clouds of noxious, thick, oily malodorous smoke are billowing straight at our house on a stiff breeze. I stump off round to remonstrate telling myself that they, in time-honoured English fashion are burning old car tyres for some reason. But no, this is the Bahamas and so they are, of course, incinerating a large quantity of old Wellington boots. I issue dark threats and the boots are duly extinguished with broad smiles all round. It is, in fact, an offence to light a bonfire in a residential area in case it sets the bush alight. Where on earth did they get them all from I ask myself and why pick here, today, to perform this bizarre funeral rite?

There are only three fire engines on the island. One is permanently tied to the airport for obvious reasons. A second, geriatric, machine languishes where it was abandoned, deep in the bush, almost intact because even it is too specialised for the locals to have worked out a way of using any of its parts they might be able to liberate. The third is in private hands on a "gated community" as an insurance discount hedge and so off limits to the common weal. Consequently, fire is a very real threat particularly during the dry winter season and because so many of the island buildings are constructed principally of wood.

In our neighbours' house wall facing the sea and the patio is an eye socket for a French window. Instead of constructing the lintel for this so that it rests with its edges in the walls to each side and can support the blocks above it, these blocks have been built up first. Water of dubious origin is used to make concrete—the sea is only five yards away. A wooden form has then been placed under the blocks and the concrete poured from hand held buckets so that the resulting lintel actually hangs from the blocks with no support whatsoever from below. If the lintel ever breaks free from the blocks in this magical ensemble the only thing stopping it from crashing to the ground will be the French window. A number of other lintels are built for the windows and doors in similar vein. We are agog.

All the corners of the house are constructed last in traditional Bahamian style. That is to say, walls are built along and up to the corner, well cured (rusted) metal "reinforcing" rods are put in place in the corner space, a form made to create the corner and concrete poured into the resulting pillar to join the two walls together—Hey presto! When the ground floor has been completed a concrete apron is poured into a form which runs the complete length of the house round the top of the walls to level them off for the commencement of the first floor build. No spirit levels needed here, not even a good "eye". Over time the first floor begins to take shape and the house rises bit by bit from the bush like some ghostly croft.

Quite fast, an enormous row breaks out between our neighbour, the contractor, the project manager and the planners. All work ceases amidst a storm of loud insults and oaths. Subsequently the builder leaves the island, for what reason we are uncertain, shortly followed by our neighbour. And the silence of doom descends on the site.

This gloomy apparition is now the focal point of the Bay, a leering, grey concrete skull, part breeze block and part overlaid cement render. Soon, nature pops in to see what can be salvaged and a jaunty casuarina takes up residence on one corner, quickly growing to six feet. Other vivacious shrubs colonise good cracks in the cement floor slab and sills and sprout exuberantly. The whole is surrounded by a pockmarked wasteland of rubble and old rusty scaffolding poles interspersed with small middens of builder's detritus. It reminds one of so many of the sad little half-built houses in Greece which look as though they have been bombed in some long forgotten vendetta by fanatical locals. We christen it "the public lavatory".

We despair of ever seeing the place completed. However, much, much later our neighbours return and under the mildly abrasive barrage of our enquiries about the public lavatory's future, assure us that a phoenix is about to rise from the ashes, if this can be said of a urinal. But to our astonishment and delight a new contractor is appointed who proves to be none other than probably the best builder on the island, by reputation.

The fairground patio is summarily demolished by back hoe in two short hours of metal rending, breeze block crunching, concrete snapping mayhem and the renaissance moves on from there. Suffice to say, the house is now an attractive asset to the Bay and we await the landscaping with hope and some confidence: Steven and Miriam have forgiven us for the temporary soubriquet of "The Public Lavatory" as this is now historical and we shall all live happily ever after, seasonally adjusted.

CHAPTER 24

Insects over here tend to be less forgiving than in the UK, foremost of which are the sand flies or biting midges called "no see 'ems" by the locals because, at the size of grains of sand they are virtually invisible and are a pest during dawn and dusk. Their bite can cause a good strong itch and enough of these can setup an allergic reaction in a susceptible human. It's annoying to realise that in the Caribbean one is part of the food chain! They are best avoided by staying indoors for the relevant hour or two in the day.

Strangely, mosquitoes are smaller here than in Europe and give a less lumpy bite. However there is, very rarely, an outside chance of getting malaria from one of these so they are best not encouraged. Most houses have insect screens (fine mesh netting) fitted to doors and windows so the problem is fairly small, nevertheless, each of our bathrooms has sprays for flying and crawling insects in the cupboards under the basins as standard equipment. There is nothing worse in a hot tropical night than to awake to the blitzkrieg whine of a dive-bombing mosquito on target. Followed by silence. But very reassuring to know that killer spray is at hand without waking the rest of the house either by having to go searching for it or using some blunt instrument in trying to swat the brute thereby simultaneously trashing the bedroom. (Just such an event was seared into my memory at a tender age by outraged, sleepy and remonstrating parents, but that is another story.)

There are snakes on the island and, very occasionally, one will come across a big 'un four or five feet long and wide to match. However, most are only two or three feet long. The good news is that, although there are ten species of snake in the Bahamas, they are all from the boa constrictor family so none is poisonous. They are all quite timid, performing a useful service by eating rodents and bugs so keeping them under control to an extent, although many locals refuse to accept this, believing that the snakes crawl into the ears of babies, eat their brains and exit through their noses. One suspects that a certain amount of voodoo influence may be pervasive; we are only 100 watery miles from Haiti, here.

Centipedes are another local delicacy. Coming in at roughly six inches long and a quarter of an inch wide, these flat, dark brown beasties (probably scalopendra polymorpha) represent an unpleasant encounter if stung by one as they are extremely toxic although not deadly. They are the very devil to kill and have the disconcerting similarity to jelly fish in that if you chop them with a spade you seem to have made two caterpillars from one. Fortunately they are fairly uncommon unless one spends a lot of time in the bush.

Similarly, scorpions are available to liven things up, on occasion. Habu is an expert at spotting them and, although a German Shepherd, he will point at one under the sofa long before anyone else spots it. They are reasonably rare, usually about an inch long, and quite slow moving so giving one a chance to deal with them before they scuttle away or damage is done. Even in this event, they are not a serious irritant at this size. The guest of a friend was putting on a pair of newly dried shorts that had been hanging on the line one day and was stung in the crotch by one; he described it as "uncomfortable" but not enough to interfere with his holiday pursuits and certainly not warranting a visit to the doctor. In fact, he seemed to be revelling in the whole drama to such an extent that we had to dissuade him from exposing himself to show us the swelling.

Expats from cooler climes will try to unnerve newcomers with tales about Tarantulas. Why this folklore persists is a mystery; there is none. What they are probably referring to is an arachnid which is known locally as a banana spider. It is indeed large, black and hairy with an unpleasant bite, but a Tarantula it is not. Other arachnids are resident although in perfectly normal quantities including, it must be admitted, the Black Widow. The Orb Web spider is particularly attractive with long legs coloured in yellow and black hoops, living on moths and other small insects that it catches in its web. However, generally speaking there are few venomous spiders in the region.

Other insects of the non toxic-variety include cockroaches. Known locally as Palmetto Bugs they grow to enormous sizes so they can make a substantially disgusting mess if squashed by way of dispatch and they are very fast. Spraying them with an insecticide is tidier in the end. Unfortunately, even the sprays from the supermarket take some time to work; initially they only slow the creatures down—pretty daunting when one's spouse is confronted with a brown-bodied bug about two and a half inches long skittering about with vast antennae waving around like a crayfish on steroids.

CHAPTER 25

Invariably, if one has any form of boat somebody will suggest water skiing sooner or later. Our friend Mike Hancock from the 'Tuscan house', so-called because it looks like one with a poplar sort of tree growing beside it, has discovered a hitherto unused set of water skis in the crannies of his bedroom cupboard and a mission is mooted. He is a fit and enthusiastic chap with an occasionally unwarranted confidence in his ability. However, not to be deterred by any 'doubting Thomasery' from us, we agree to meet Mike and his wife Judy at the boatyard around noon. The plan is to do some skiing and then potter down island, find a deserted beach and have a picnic.

The engine on our boat is a decent 115 horsepower Suzuki but although the boat is only 18feet long it is built for lake fishing so it is a sturdy platform. We express some mild reservations about its pulling power but these are brushed aside. The programme will continue as planned: there will be no problems. Skis, tow rope, flippers, snorkels, picnic cool boxes, towels and clothes bags are all loaded aboard followed by the humans.

We leave the mooring jetties in Victoria Pond, motor across to sheltered, shallow water beside Stocking Island and tip the enthusiast into the sea with his skis. After a period of fine-tuning adjustment he signals that he is ready so we power up the boat. As we feared, the bow of the boat swoops up whilst the stern digs in. Our intrepid skier is dragged along in a semi-foetal position producing a massive bow wave. His expression is glazed but determined, like a boxer after the second knockdown and he is swallowing gallons of salt sea water which is pumping at hydraulic pressure up his nostrils. Unbeknown to us he is also receiving an oceanic enema. Finally he gesticulates at us to stop so, taking pity on him, we turn to haul him and the skis back on the boat. He wants to say something but can only manage "glub, glub". We repeat the exercise at his insistence.

Eventually, when he can speak after another inter-orifices douche we all agree that it is high time for the second part of the adventure to proceed down island for snorkelling and a picnic. I throttle up the engine and off we go. After a little while his face takes on a haunted look and a distinctly, green, bilious hue. He asks plaintively "Is it far?" "Not really". "It's just that I'm feeling rather sea-sick". Out of sympathy for an ailing passenger who is looking quite pallid we stop at a little beach on the way down for him to recover. We wade ashore, lay out the towels, commencing the ritual sun-cream anointment. Meanwhile, he has squatted in the water so that only his head and torso are visible leaving us to wonder what he is up to. Eventually he scuttles out of the water to lie in the sun to a chorus of frivolous, not to say undignified, comment and suggestion. After a moment, however, he leaps up feverishly clutching his buttocks—it seems he has been stung a number of times. And a return to the water for a good scratch to cool off his bottom is the poor man's only solution. The subject of hosting water skiing again has been notable by its absence since a diplomatic silence now enshrouds this event. We go snorkelling instead.

oooooooo0ooooooooo

Many of the natives of Exuma have an inbuilt aversion to work ably assisted by sun, rum, fun and a certain indolence. Unlike the residents of Britain this has nothing to do with the welfare state but is a strong desire to avoid the historical slur of slavery, working in menial jobs. Most of the island opportunities fall into this category as tourism provides some seventy percent of the economy. In the 1980s Exumans received a vast infusion of wealth from an unexpected source, drugs. The island was the most northern point that a twin-engined plane from Colombia could reach without refuelling, making it an ideal staging post for the USA. The islanders turned to moving the product along with alacrity, making enormous fortunes very quickly as a result. Even allowing for fisherman's exaggeration the stories of fast sports cars and extravagant limousines pouring into the docks at George Town to be driven in a land with no metalled roads are fascinating. Cars were the preferred means of banking and their boots were stuffed full of cash as the owners were fearful that putting it into an account would alert the authorities. Wise souls maintained a "real job" so that they had a visible means of income when the police or customs came calling; more foolish virgins paraded their new found wealth and numbers of them ended up in jail at the US president's convenience when the inevitable clean-up got under way. To this day, one discovers in conversation that a number of upright pillars of the local community have done "time" for drugs in the past.

Nowadays the US Drug Enforcement Agency has a permanent presence and helicopter patrols regularly criss-cross the island as a deterrent, although we understand that these movements are logged and certain people informed of the flight path by mobile phone immediately on take-off. Drug smuggling, no longer a significant source of income, has been superseded by the more healthy funds of tourism. Nevertheless, it is surprising how often one comes across a "road" deep in the bush which starts and ends nowhere and, given the jungle's propensity for winning back territory, it is interesting how well cut back, to the width of a light plane's wingspan, these seem to be so long after the supposed end of the drug era.

CHAPTER 26

Tourists come to the Bahamas for many reasons but one of the most consistent is fishing. Game and other species include great barracuda, amberjack, bluefin tuna, marlin, bonefish, mahi mahi (dolphin), grouper, snapper, sailfish, kingfish and wahoo. The big ticket event in Exuma is the bonefishing: bonefish, I am told provide the best sport of all. There are plenty of boats and experienced skippers for hire or if you are feeling adventurous you can wade up the flats on the "south side" of the island casting as you go, although it is as well to remember that out here you, also, are part of the food chain.

Great Barracuda (Sphyreana barracuda) are an attraction both as food and game fish. Growing up to 6ft long with an under bite full of viciously sharp fang-like teeth of different sizes similar to Piranhas, they are well-designed voracious, opportunistic predators who will eat other fish as big as themselves if necessary, by tearing off hunks of flesh. They rely on surprise and speed to kill, travelling at up to 27 miles per hour to overtake prey. Although not normally interested in humans or dogs they can be attracted by jewellery and splashing so that even two or four legs paddling in 18 inches of water can be enough for a mistaken view that a target fish is in distress and produce an attack. These are rare but do happen: an acquaintance of ours needed 12 stitches in her lower leg in identical circumstances paddling on the south side last year.

Not surprisingly if one is swimming, fish to avoid include the occasional barracuda, lion fish which have colourful but toxic spines, and sharks for obvious reasons.

There is something mildly unnerving about swimming along and becoming aware that one is being watched. A swivel around in the water confirms that a barracuda is on station, usually about ten feet away. The thing about them is that their scales are such a colour of grey/silver that they appear translucent from the side view merely reflecting their surroundings and their shadow on the sea bed is all that gives them away, otherwise they are virtually invisible. Once you've got one, where ever you go it goes; try turning towards it and it will merely retreat, maintaining its distance. They are quite short-sighted but extremely curious creatures and can spoil a leisurely swim or snorkel by this stalking technique.

Lion fish are much smaller and not such a problem for humans; although they can be aggressive they sit more or less stationary by rock outcrops and so unless one of their spines is accidentally touched for any reason they can be ignored. The trouble is that they are a Pacific species which was unintentionally introduced to the Caribbean in the 1990s. They have since become invasive and consume large quantities of small, pretty reef fish decimating these colonies swiftly. They have few predators other than man but they are taken by tiger grouper and moray eels on occasion. In some parts of the Caribbean there is now a bounty on them and efforts are being made to create recipes for their succulent white flesh with the assurance that they are perfectly safe if the fins are avoided during preparation. Sounds compelling but we have not tried this and it may well be outside our culinary comfort zone.

The Bahamas are home to a number of species of shark. The principal varieties are the lemon, the bull and the nurse shark.

Lemons are usually 8-10 feet long and are bottom feeders with poor eyesight but have very accurate magnetic sensors in the nose.

Putting risk in perspective, there have been a mere 22 recorded attacks on humans since 1580 with no recorded deaths.

Bulls are well known for their aggressive and unpredictable behaviour and can grow up to 11ft. They have a high tolerance of fresh water and can be found in rivers many miles from the ocean, not a problem in the Bahamas. They are solitary hunters whose diet consists of bony fish and other sharks but can also include dolphins, turtles, birds and other mammals. They often live in very shallow waters, which makes them one of the most dangerous species to humans and are also the shark species most likely to attack them. One reportedly attacked a race horse in Australia! Mercifully, these are rarely seen in our waters.

Nurse sharks are quite prevalent, especially up the Cays but are pretty much harmless to humans.

It would be remiss whilst on the subject of sharks not to point out that migrating whale sharks can be seen in the Atlantic between Exuma and Long Island during the months of March and April. These enormous and gentle giants are the biggest fish on Earth. They feed on plankton and can grow to 40 feet, about the size of a single-decker bus. If you manage to get into the water with one you had better be fit because they swim lazily at some considerable speed.

For anyone with a slightly different bent the sea abounds with lobster (crayfish) and conch. Both of these are part of the island's staple diet although to our way of thinking the crayfish are not as tasty as the North Sea lobster.

ooooooooOoooooooo

The Exuma Cays are surrounded by a spectacular natural aquarium containing an abundance of marine life but are themselves out of bounds for fishing purposes, having been established as the Exuma Land and Sea Park managed by the Bahamas National Trust. Amongst other animals of interest the Cays are host to several rare and endangered species of iguanas and the curly tailed lizard.

One of the highlights of any visit to the island has to be a trip up the Cays and our favourite skipper for the trip is Peter Burrows a big, genial and laid back Bahamian with the consummate knowledge of local flora, fauna and reef conditions that goes with the territory. Usually starting at Barreterre, a charming fishing village of little multicoloured cottages at the northern tip of Exuma, boats leave early for the day trip. On the outward bound journey a stop at Little Guana Cay is a must to see the Iguanas which are a critically endangered species. These lizards are between 2 and 3 feet long and look like something out of Chinese mythology with their strange almost bird-like pointed heads, red and orange scales, crested backs and tails. As curious about us as we are about them, they plod lazily over the beach to get a better view when we arrive. They seem singularly pedestrian, however a big surprise awaits us for several latecomers appear on the cliff top at the rear of the beach and proceed to launch themselves down the perpendicular cliff head-first joining the others, not one bit abashed, for a better look at us.

Also of note is the "German Castle," a substantial house now in ruins on Big Darby with a long concrete jetty at the water's edge which was apparently used during the Second World War as a refuge and revictualling station for German U boats. The path from the jetty to the house is now substantially overgrown with poisonwood trees aplenty, which adds a certain 'frisson' to the exploration.

Next up is a visit to Big Major Cay the home of the swimming pigs. The fascination that this particular spectacle holds for many, including L, has always eluded me. Nevertheless, these are a family of feral pigs which live on the Cay and swim out to the boat for scraps of vegetables that are dropped over the side for them as they paddle around the hull. The little porkers, for they are not large as pigs go, have white coats with brown patches They look like any other pigs to me but it must be allowed that I'm not a pig connoisseur.

At Compass Cay one gets the chance to actually swim with sharks which is pretty exciting by any standards. The sharks in question are Nurse sharks which are used to the staff at the little marina throwing in a few morsels of frankfurter sausage to attract their attention. They swarm round the jetty waiting for more and are fairly oblivious to any humans who happen to be in the water with them. Nurse sharks are bottom feeders although they live happily in shallow waters. They are nocturnal and spend the day inactive in clusters but are solitary hunters growing to in excess of 10ft, except for the ones at Compass! They eat mostly small shellfish by crushing them with their toothless jaws. And this is the thing, it is a good idea to keep fingers and toes out of range when they are feeding—they look surprisingly like frankfurters when you stop to consider it. But it is a quite special experience having these creatures brushing past as they swim around.

Lunch is usually taken at one of the waterside bars or restaurants on Staniel, Sampson or Compass Cay.

Close to Staniel Cay lies Thunderball Grotto featured in a number of films, most particularly the James Bond movie of the same name. This is a spectacular under sea cave which provides unrivalled diving and snorkelling opportunities. But, of course, the first thing to do after swimming through one of the several entrances (at low tide for snorkelers) is to look up and wonder at the natural sky-light hole in the ceiling of the cave which allows the light to stream in; nature did it before Michelangelo and St Peter's Basilica! One is surrounded by a kaleidoscope of fish shoals both inside the cave and beyond its northern exit, the latter achieved by allowing the current to sweep one round the tip of the island back to the boat when the tide is running right.

By the time one returns to Exuma one feels tired and fulfilled with inevitable tales of sights seen and the beauty of nature.

The time we went up Peter, the boat owner, wanted to stay at Staniel Cay for the weekend so he threw in a flight back from there to Exuma at the end of the day which was extremely civilised. We piled into Steve Smith Charters' smart little five seater but as we were taxiing up the runway to start our take off, blow me if a cheeky little Cessna didn't pull out immediately in front of us (we had to brake) and, queue-barging, took off in front of us. A traffic jam on the runway—only in the Bahamas!

CHAPTER 27

The bat moth is a species that is striking, if nocturnal. Otherwise known locally as the money moth, it has a wing span of sometimes as much as nine inches. If disturbed during the evening these large, black, beautiful, harmless creatures will flutter off into the darkness unnerving people new to the island who resolve to take a little more water with it until explanations are supplied. The moths can often be seen resting up in the shade of a verandah or roof overhang during the day but they are quite shy and need to be approached with care so as not to frighten them away. As with many species of Lepidoptera their wings bear beautifully intricate patterns in burnt umber on close inspection.

Exuma has a number of native and migratory birds. These include egrets, banana quits and feral peafowl. Ospreys nest and hatch young during the spring rearing them in vast scruffy nests of tree branches, lengths of old rope, fishing net and any other detritus that catches their attention. Given the opportunity, they will return to the same spot each year and build another 'squat' on top of the previous nest. They are an inspiring sight when they glide, often in pairs or, later, in families along the shoreline thermals on the lookout for fish. Often the first indication of their presence is their high keening cry which compels one to look skywards to locate its source.

Spring is also the time when the laughing gulls arrive. Woe betide anyone who has left the bimini sunshade up on his boat down at the boatyard. They become the target for flocks of gulls who lounge around on them squabbling, fighting and laying down a goodly layer of guano, cackling their heads off all the while. Trying to perform any intricate activity on one's boat is frustrating enough as it rocks on the water but is even more so when an audience of gulls is perched adjacent apparently hooting and falling about in rapturous merriment at one's efforts. Hands become all thumbs while spanners, screwdrivers etc develop a magnetic attraction to the water, dropping over the side with unwarranted ease.

Greater anis (Crotophaga major) are resident all year round. Although members of the cuckoo family these birds look like big crows with blue glossed black plumage, a long spatulate tail and the head and beak of a parrot. They tumble about the bushes in rumbustious gangs encouraging each other with a distinctive 'keee, keee' call.

The tiny humming birds are a joy to watch as they plunder the hibiscus blossoms and Pride of Barbados flowers with their long delicate beaks, their wings beating so fast they hum distinctively all the while. The sea grape in the front garden that shelters us from the ocean is a favourite haunt for little blue and little green herons which look for small hermit crabs and break the shells, searching for exactly the right piece of ground and placing them reverentially before delivering a devastating downward dive of the beak. However the method is very often unsuccessful so one can watch them trundling round the bushes doing this with total absorption for half an hour or more, the loud crack of beak on shell making for an interrupted afternoon siesta on the verandah.

Breakfast is a theatre watching the ground-doves, little round tufty rusty blue things and mourning doves with a smart white collar pottering round below looking for bugs in the sand between visits to the bird bath.

One of the more unusual animals found in the Bahamas is the land crab of which there are four different species. While living on land it is aquatic by nature and needs sea water for the salt. It burrows deep holes in the mangroves or near the sea so that it can be level with the water table which must be brackish at the least. When the time comes to deposit its eggs the females head for the sea and lay them immersed in the water using their gills to breathe. They are quite nervous bodies and nocturnal so one is unlikely to bump into one during the day. Principally vegetarian they will only eat carrion if necessary. They can grow to a good size with the main claw reaching 12 inches and the leg spread measuring 18. Having said this, on the internet I have seen a picture of a land crab clinging to the side of a dustbin and it is the same size as the dustbin! Not for me on a dark night, thank you—the claw looks as though it would take one's leg off. As the eggs and the crabs are edible they are prized by the locals.

Distinct from the land crabs is the Caribbean hermit crab which lives in an empty shell which it discards for a larger one as it grows to full size, normally somewhere near the size of a fist. It has a large red/purple right claw which it uses to seal the entrance to its shell after retreating within when attacked. We often find them pottering unsuspectingly around the garden; they seem unable to look upwards too well so one can surprise them quite easily.

There are three species of sting ray—the eagle ray, a large mollusc eater but harmless to humans, the southern stingray and the yellow stingray which has tail barbs with venom glands causing discomfort but rarely concern.

The southern sting ray is the most common variety found in the Bahamas. It has a greyish brown topside which makes ideal camouflage on the sandy ocean floor. It is not poisonous, only using its tail barbs in defence. The most common injury arising from these creatures results from stepping on the barbs of a ray half-buried in the sand: they are extremely difficult to see once they are dug in, but these injuries are rare in practice. A great pleasure is to watch them gliding gracefully across the sand in shallow water; it's a constant source of wonder that they move so swiftly and, of course, in complete silence. This last may seem a peculiar remark but somehow one expects something that large (they are usually not less that a metre in diameter and can grow as large as two) to make some noise! They eat small crabs, worms and fish. At Chat 'n' Chill, the beach bar on Stocking Island, the rays are fed once a day so one can stand in the sea calf deep and be caressed by them as they swoop gently around looking for morsels to hoover up.

Although jelly fish are rare off Exuma, Portuguese Men of War are occasional visitors to Bahamian waters with hanging tentacles as long as 80 feet. Poison discharged by these can be lethal to humans.

Trees and shrubs include lignum vitae, coco plum, yellow elder, buttonwood, mangroves black, white and red, palms, gum elemi, strong back (Bourreria ovata), royal poinciana, australian pine (casuarina), bottlebrush, sea grape, tamarind, sapodilla, sugar apple, custard apple, soursop, guava, banana, avocado, paw paw and breadfruit. Inevitably, some have names appropriate to their function or appearance. Thus buttonwoods were named because the branches were suited to being cut up for buttons.

The casuarina, locally also known as ironwood for its hardness, was originally introduced to the Bahamas to act as a wind break tree and is now regarded as an invasive species. The name arises from the Malay word for the cassowary 'kasuari' because of the similarities between the bird's feathers and the tree's foliage. It now stands accused of destroying the limestone with its roots, burrowing deep into, and splitting, the rock apart as well as asphyxiating any plant growth beneath it. Nevertheless, pruned at a short height it bushes and can make a handsome hedge or specimen shrub.

Poisonwood is a member of the sumac family. Metopium toxiferum to give it its latin name has, as the name implies highly toxic sap containing urushiol which attacks the nervous system and causes a rash on the skin after the slightest contact. In cases of smoke inhalation it damages the lungs which is another good reason for not burning garden/bush refuse as most people cannot identify young poisonwood saplings and so do not know what not to put on the fire.

With all that tropical warmth and all those beautiful Caribbean maidens sexual performance is never far from the mind of a Bahamian and 'strong back' is named for its allegedly aphrodisiac qualities, to be taken as tea by the male of the species before an athletic evening out.

Manchineel is a rarely found tree, which has poisonous green fruit and toxic latex. Rain water or dew from these trees brought into contact with the eyes can cause temporary blindness.

CHAPTER 28

Gambling is generally encouraged for non residents particularly in Nassau the Bahamas capital, although Exuma's casino is closed for lack of punters. Locals are prohibited from gambling under penalty of fines or up to six months imprisonment. But get close if you can, by avoiding the picket/lookout sentry, to where and when they are playing dominoes and take a bet on who, if anybody, is not gambling!

ooooooooOooooooooo

One of the Bahamas' very special events is Junkanoo, a unique fiesta, the Bahamian equivalent to Mardi Gras or Rio de Janeiro's carnival. The origins of the name are uncertain but theories include the corruption of the name of an instigating slave Johnnie Canoe or the French "gens inconnus" because the revellers faces are covered by masks and so are unknown. Unlike its carnival cousins Junkanoo is not linked to Lent and takes place on Boxing Day morning with, in Exuma, the start scheduled for 2am, which is an opportunity for all, but particularly the islanders, to extend the Christmas celebrations with yet more rum and festivity; it is hot, after all. This does not seem to be a problem for many folk but after a Christmas Day of celebration and gross over indulgence I find I can feel as bilious as the best of them. My head badly needs sleep, my heart seems to be racing having overdosed on calories and sugar and my stomach is revolting. Having turned up at the appointed time in this febrile state on two occasions we realise belatedly that, of course, this is the Bahamas so the actual fun will begin at four. This is civilised; with strong will one can rise at three thirty, drawn by the call of the distant drums, to be booted and spurred in time for the action.

During the interim the three competing teams will have built enormous fires around which sit their drumming cadres warming their drum-skins to loosen them up to the right pitch. The drums cover the spectrum from small snare drums through medium size tomtoms to enormous things made from plastic oil drums supported by a thick sash slung across the drummer's shoulder and round his neck. Each drumming section plays a different rhythm which creates the overall hypnotic and compelling but slightly unnerving tribal sound. The fiesta involves each team in turn parading along the strip of the Queen's Highway beside the George Town administrative building. Astonishing floats covering diverse themes (religion, gambling, independence) made extravagantly and inventively out of crepe paper and cardboard lit by portable generators at the back are followed by troupes of brightly dressed dancers all swaying and leaping to the beat of the band behind—a brass section blowing their cheeks off with added bells and cow horns followed by the corps of drummers beating out the tribal rhythms in a sweat of effort and concentration bringing up the rear. The smallest drums are the snares, probably borrowed from one or other church's Sunday drum set. Then come the tomtoms. Beyond these are the 'big boys' with the converted plastic oil drums. Their rhythms are so visceral that it is impossible to avoid the instinctive urge to tap one's feet at the least: many cannot resist the temptation to dance and join the rear ranks of the parade. The floats and head-dresses will have taken most of the year to make but will be destroyed after the parade.

The last pass of the teams is at about 7am by which time the dawn has come and the clear blue sky promises another beautiful sunny day in paradise. Having seen everyone and talked to them all at length on most subjects, particularly which team had the best floats, dancers, band etc so that all us experts will be confounded as usual when the winners are announced, the groups of revellers begin to disperse for bed. We think a leisurely breakfast followed by a leisurely day's boating and picnicking is in order.

ooooooooOooooooooo

After a supper of tomato (our own) and basil (also our own) salad with seared tuna steak, we are off to Eddie's Edgewater, it being Monday night. As the name implies, Eddie's is a bar on the edge of the Victoria Pond opposite where all the sheltered moorings and jetties lie. Every Monday evening, and tonight is no exception, there is live music in the form of the local, traditional "rake and scrape" band. In concept they are quite similar to the UK skiffle groups of the 1950s and play mostly uptempo calypso. There are approximately six musicians depending on who has strolled to the bar for a beer or gone off for a bop and they are mostly 'plugged', as opposed to 'unplugged'. One of these plays a handsaw with an old screwdriver; there is also a guitarist and a keyboards player; a standard drum set is complemented by two further drummers each on the big Junkanoo oil-drums (not to be confused with the tin-pans which in the UK we know as 'steel drums') and a singer. Completing the ensemble is the only white face in the line-up who plays the "gut and bucket"—an instrument comprising a large metal bucket with a broom handle jammed into it. A single string passes from the edge of the bucket to the top of the broom handle and flexing the handle allows for tension to be varied on the string creating a (limited) tonal range. An earful of Eddie's rake and scrape is a good way to banish any hint of Monday blues (yes, even in Exuma that lifelong psychological gremlin occasionally reasserts itself!) and should not be a late night.

ooooooooOooooooooo

It has been a beautiful day. The sea has been flat calm so we have been out on the boat for a swim and picnic lunch on "our beach" so called because we never meet anyone else on it. The sky has been clear apart from some strands of stratus and the sun has been hot. On our return L spots that the parsley by the front door has had a nasty turn and is lying wilting over the edge of its flower pot. A terse and faintly demoralising debate ensues about my perceived skills at watering; it is a known fact that under my myopic care the new potatoes we were propagating expired from drought and on pain of torture I am not allowed to go anywhere near the tomatoes. Later we have some guests for drinks and during the course of the evening one wanders off to the loo in the utility room. Much later, after they have left I go there too but am mildly nonplussed to find that the wash basin is overflowing with a jungly profusion of aggressively rehabilitated parsley, rendering ablutions quite impossible. I pause for a moment to consider what our guest must have thought when confronted by this foliage fiesta.

Afterwards we drive down to a Gospel Choir Competition being run in Regatta Park, a small plot of sun-weary grass with an outdoor stage in George Town. This has been organised by the "Beautify the Fish Fry" committee in aid of tidying up the area around the fish fry shacks to encourage the tourists to investigate, eat and drink there. Presumably, the tourists are currently too timid to overcome the occasional swooping supermarket bag and odd destitute plastic cup riffling in the breeze and join in the loud, boisterous fun that the Fish Fry has to offer and get a chance to meet the locals at play. The competition runs from 5 until 8. We pass originally at 5 on the way back from the boat but the Park is deserted. At 6.30 our guests pass by, ringing us to say that the situation is unchanged. Eventually we go down again at 7.45 on the grounds that everything Bahamian is always hours late, to discover that none of the five choirs scheduled to sing has turned up and the whole event has been a complete fiasco—"Only in the Bahamas," we sigh. So we slope off to Charlie's our favourite shack and have delicious garlic prawns, coleslaw, potato salad, lettuce, tomatoes and a plastic cup or two of wine.

CHAPTER 29

Today, driving up the Queen's Highway, I fall in behind a classic scenario. It is an ancient Chevrolet pick-up truck travelling at 30 miles an hour in a 45mph limit zone but as the road is twisty at this point I am unable to overtake. The truck's rotting muffler (silencer) which is held on by two pieces of rusting wire joggles in an ominously cheerful manner as the vehicle heaves and clatters from one side of the road to the other wheezing and sputtering over the frequent bumps and potholes. The tailgate appears to be seized up at the hinges which are secured at their tops by bent screwdrivers threaded through the lugs on either side. The bald rear tyres roll along encouraging the flapping stub residues of the long-shredded mudflaps. The truck is left hand drive despite the rule being drive on the left, as in the UK. The driver is so relaxed he has slid down the seat and is almost lost from view; only the top of his baseball cap indicates occupancy other than a languid right hand resting on the top of the steering wheel. His left arm hangs limply out of the driver's window twitching spasmodically on the door panel below where it performs a sort of natural ventilation with the palm of the hand held open against the breeze created by the truck's movement. We begin to slow down without apparent reason and still no prospect of passing. It is a warm afternoon and I wonder if, perhaps, he has nodded off. As the locals frequently drive themselves into a catatonic state I am unconcerned. However, at the last minute emergency braking is applied without benefit of brake lights and the dead arm jerks into life, rising zombie-like to point over the roof at the other side of the road. Sure enough, a concealed cart-track has emerged and the truck veers sharp right and, in a sudden frenetic burst of speed, hurtles up it disappearing in a Saharan dust cloud as though pursued by the hounds of Hell. Silence falls; mercifully the road ahead is deserted.

oooooooo0ooooooooo

We are going down to the supermarket in George Town to replenish our supplies of ciabattas and olives now that we know the supply boat has come in. Coming up on a school bus from behind we notice the legend "Danger, this school bus stops at all railway crossings". This on an island which doesn't even have a single traffic light let alone a railway. The answer is straightforward; the buses are bought or otherwise acquired second-hand from the States thus bearing the livery of the school they originally served. When they have completed their allotted span here they are driven to the south end of the island where there is a sort of elephants' graveyard in which old buses lie being slowly consumed by the bush, every cranny sprouting vines and other flora in profusion.

oooooooo0ooooooooo

We have been misled! There is a handsome tree in our garden which the builders did not sacrifice and locals have told us it is a "kamomilly" tree. Requesting a spelling we are told "Chamomile" which surprises us because we thought that this was a lawn plant. But we do know that they make tea out of it so we accept the information at face value. Then we hear it pronounced "Gamomilly" so I am finally driven to research it only to discover that it is in fact a "Gum elemi" tree (Bursera simaruba). With red peeling bark it is also locally known for obvious reasons as the "Tourist Tree". The bark is much prized for its medicinal qualities, boiled in the form of bush tea, which allegedly relieves fever, aches and pains. Its other local name is the "Fence Post Tree" because new trees can be grown merely by sticking branches into the soil to make living fences for livestock and property. That said, the best example I know of surrounds a domino den in George Town and keeps the participants well cordoned off from prying policemen.

We have had to prune our tree because it is gobbling up our best view (shrubs and trees can easily put on eight feet of growth in a season down here.) So we are going to try the fence concept down one side of the garden. These trees will grow to a decent size (35 feet locally and, potentially, 90ft or more) and are semi-deciduous with small creamy white flowers but most importantly they are drought, wind and salt tolerant, a pretty formidable combination in these parts. It is, apparently, the traditional wood used for carousel horses in the United States and the sap can be used for glue, varnish and incense.

ooooooooo0ooooooooo

Percy Fox our favourite, wily realtor is the man who sold us our land, eventually. He is also one of the island's Justices of the Peace and a charming rogue. On visiting him to discuss property matters we find that he is planning to retire. As he has been closely involved in island affairs for so many years L asks him what he will do to fill his time. Percy's response is unequivocal, "At my time of life, my dear, believe me I can watch paint dry!"

Our friends Mike and Judy, who own the "Tuscan villa", never wear watches on the island and are consequently, un-Englishly, late for everything. This is a malaise that affects a number of expats and great numbers of locals. The current edition of our local newspaper endorses this, carrying an interesting article on local crime. It says, ". . . . Among the challenges for police, is solving the John Bull jewellery shop robbery in which two masked gunmen got away with a quantity of Rolex watches". Police are confident of apprehending the villains—finding two Exumans who can actually tell them the time should do the trick.

ooooooooOoooooooo

This evening we are having friends Simon and Cynthia and family for drinks. They have parents-in-law together with a cousin and husband staying and it is customary to "help out" occasionally with other folks' guests. We all sit on the verandah in the balmy breeze and admire a full moon laying a silver fairy path over the sea from Stocking Island opposite back across to us. The mast-head lights of a dozen moored yachts twinkle at us from the lee of the island. Everything is sublimely bathed in moonlight.

But the time comes to leave this magical scene and we all pile off to the Exuma Fish Fry for breaded shrimp and barbecue ribs at Charlie's shack. After supper with, plainly, too much wine Steve, the owner of Charlie's, lights up his Karaoke and all have a go. In my opinion this is an instrument of the Devil. The evening now deteriorates very swiftly and we are back home for bed by 10.45.

CHAPTER 30

Driving to the supermarket the other day I was delighted to add to my collection of wayside experiences the sight of a car stationary on the roadside with a large goat loitering on its boot lid. Only in the Bahamas (and Crete).

Opposite Smittys, our little local "supermarket" a small quarry has been disused for some time and has become the resting and rusting place of some automobilia. Up against the rock wall at the rear are parked two ancient vehicles, a dirty sand yellow tarmac wagon and a similarly liveried smallish tanker, both in the process of being subsumed back into the bush as brilliant green shrubs and creepers begin their reclamation. In the exciting prospect of a general election this year the FNM (Free National Movement) party erect their Exuma headquarters on the quarry site. Consumed by enthusiasm beyond normal Exuman bounds the building is constructed at the back of the site immediately in front of the two decaying monsters thereby consigning them, for our huge enjoyment, to a permanent resting place—there being no space to manoeuvre forward or backward to escape. However, our pleasure is short lived for a few days later, in an uncharacteristic flurry of pragmatism, an operational, yellow, monster crane arrives on site and drags them unceremoniously sideways to freedom leaving a large scar in the ground where they and the resurgent jungle had been. Very disappointing.

Just further north along the Queen's Highway lies what must be one of the smallest houses on the island: from the look of it, only two rooms and a tiny deck and loggia. Hanging from the centre of the loggia is a sign of precocious brio proclaiming proudly that it is the head office of "The Colossal Construction Company". We have never seen any evidence of this corporate behemoth on the island, not even the usual tatty old rusting pickup truck, the preferred mode of transport for most of Exuman builders. Marketing is in short supply for contractors' names apart from the above, ranging from "Caribbean Construction Co" (a one-horse operation) and "Rowdy Boys Construction" to the biblical "Upon This Rock Construction Co".

ooooooooOooooooo

As with all underdeveloped but expanding places the island of Exuma is slowly sinking under a plethora of voluntary committees. The most recent of which goes by the obscure title of the "Beautify the Fish Fry Committee" (purpose; to increase the attraction of our fish and chip shack village to tourists). The main committee has already spawned two offspring, the "Fundraising Committee" to find the money to beautify and the "Construction Committee" to build septic tanks and lavatories for each shack. At present there are some unspeakably gruesome outside privies at one end of the site where carnivorous mosquitoes the size of horses dive bomb any exposed flesh in squadrons.

I have escaped these committees but for my sins have been ensnared onto the Exuma Building Information Committee (inevitable acronym EBIC) whose purpose is to provide data to stop new arrivals on the island from being ripped off by spurious builders and other assorted raptors in the food chain. It is, however, chaired by one of the island's expat "project managers" which renders its impartiality somewhat dubious. I am also on the Tennis Club Development Committee with lofty ideals but no money. At present we are receiving quotations from tennis court contractors in Nassau, there being none on the island. In the main these estimates are masterpieces of those two imposters obfuscation and bifurcation so clarity of purpose is in inverse proportion to the numbers of quotations received.

ooooooooOooooooooo

Last week was an impressive one for the accident tally and included a lorry with a large crane on it. It must have left the Queen's Highway at speed and ended up slewed over on the beach. Later and more spectacularly, a car left the Highway and overshot the beach altogether and having executed a 180° turn came to rest up to its windscreen in the ocean with the boot facing seawards and the bonnet facing land. Bahamian drivers generally escape these death defying adventures completely unharmed. The level of alcohol in the blood stream renders them rubbery so that they emerge floppy but cheerfully uninjured. Overhearing the culprit relaying the incident is entertaining; after a number of calls to chums (all locals have mobile phones) the grin tends to spread as they begin to enjoy the frisson of their achievement.

ooooooooOooooooooo

The Bahamas Music and Heritage Festival takes place this weekend. Three days and more importantly three nights of choirs, bands, partying and revelry sponsored by the Tourist Board together with the usual suspects—local liquor stores, banks, insurance companies, electricity, water and telecoms companies and an airline or two. To do them justice most of these organisations, to their great credit, put their hands in their pockets for every conceivable island event.

The Festival Bar is set up on Regatta Park, a small and for the moment enshrouded area with a wooden stage in the middle of George Town: black plastic sheeting has been erected around the Park's periphery fence to stop those who are enthusiastic but penniless (or mean) from seeing the acts free of charge. Later, the entrance and ticket booth will be manned by some cheerful but heavy dudes. The Bar is open all day and folk drift in and out of the Park to buy tee shirts, baseball caps and other memorabilia. There are displays of conch shell and woodcarving, model boat building, straw plaiting, jewellery and bread making. Competitions include onion peeling, conch cracking, kite flying, hoola hooping and coconut barking. Story telling for the children also features.

From 6pm until 8 the place is eerily quiet as the island prepares itself to party. This involves gallons of perfume and aftershave plus very tight trousers, jeans, skirts and glitzy tops for the women to show themselves to the best advantage. The men appear to make rather less effort, as one might expect.

The first evening is taken up with a sedate selection of the island's gospel choirs supported by some visiting talent.

At 8pm on Friday officially and 8.45 actually, the first act of the evening in the local talent category bursts into action. By 9 Audley Dames and the Sweet Love Band are laying down some storming calypso. 10 until 12 is the visiting artists section and apart from the bands the enthusiastic crowd is treated to an exhibition of Junkanoo drumming and a limbo dancer with the inevitable flaming pole. This he negotiates safely, rendering superfluous the traditional midnight execution for failure at this by a participating slave. Nassau band Tingem Dem lead and back various Bahamian artists until 2am when a heavily fuelled crowd receive the Junkanoo rush out for half an hour to much acclaim. (the rush out is an abbreviated carnival procession of masked musicians and drummers beating out African rhythms to which the crowd dances adding whistles, cow bells and anything else which comes to hand.)

9am Saturday. After a short night broken by a monstrous thunderstorm, tennis has been organised. We present ourselves wearily for two hours of mixed doubles which does nothing to alleviate the slight pain behind the eyes and the mild but persistent sense of nausea which is likely to prevail for the rest of the day until some form of remedy is taken.

As exhaustion beckons, the third night of Festival, which is basically a repeat of night two with different acts, is not a runner and we agree to meet friends for supper in the early evening at the dock. We consume a large resuscitative rum and coke before setting out. On arrival it seems that our chums have had a similar idea because they are dispensing Margaritas from the boot of their car while we all wait for the ferry. We embark in high spirits to cross Queen Elizabeth Harbour for an al fresco meal at St Francis' restaurant on Stocking Island with its panoramic view of the anchored boats and George Town's lights twinkling on the inky water.

We return at 9pm and after coffee retire to bed by 10. At midnight we are roused from slumber by, seemingly, a ship's broadside. Leaping in shock onto the verandah to discover the source of the noise, it is swiftly apparent that the Festival close is a spectacularly deafening fireworks display which we watch for 20 minutes before finally returning to bed.

Awaking on Sunday all is quiet. This morning, impressively, no cars have been abandoned by their drivers in ditches, trees or the ocean—a considerable accolade for the Festival.

On a previous, memorable occasion twelve cars parked down one side of the road into George Town had all been squeezed thinner by a gentleman who was so overwrought by the open bars that he had driven past the cars bouncing off each one in turn to maintain direction and keep himself on the road.

CHAPTER 31

Today we go to Nassau—a red letter day because it is only the third time I have been "off island" since we moved here to live and I'm beginning to get a slight case of cabin fever or islanditis as it is known locally. We rise pre-dawn at 5am to catch the 7.39am flight leaving Habu to be looked after by our kind friend Bill for the day. After 4 days of tropical rain the day breaks with sunshine and fluffy trade-wind clouds, which bodes well. The flight is uneventful apart from being full of enormous Bahamians who are all far too big for the seats. We feel positively Lilliputian beside them and wonder why the aircraft has not been fitted for purpose. We arrive with, ominously, a large empty suitcase to be filled and some paintings to be mounted and framed. We meet our driver without a hitch; she is the sister of an Exuman so we are practically related. A driver is not only cheaper than a day-taxi but also much less stressful than a hire car in Nassau's gridlock traffic.

We set off for a garden centre looking for furniture and narrowly avoid buying a large ceramic amphora because the glaze is crazed, and some wind chimes. A kaleidoscope of other shops and retail opportunities pass by and it is time for lunch. We locate the Café La Matisse opposite the Parliament buildings, sinking thankfully into chairs at a cool, palm shaded table in the garden. The Matisse is, confusingly, an Italian restaurant and a favourite watering hole for MPs, legal eagles and business folk, but none the worse for that. Indeed it makes for a fascinating passeggiata as we try to guess who is who and up to what. The staff are immaculately dressed in spotless ironed white shirts and silk ties! I cannot remember when I last saw someone wearing a decent tie. The menu is anticipatory and the wine list comprehensive. We have a delicious lunch with a good bottle of wine. The only slight disappointment is when a basin of Muscat on offer with ricotta cheese cake and strawberries in hot chocolate proves to be illusory—Nassau has run out of Muscat. Probably just as well given the prospect of more arduous shopping to come.

So onward we march, arriving at our final garden centre where we buy a teak table for our verandah and, of course, a large 3 foot long Mexican ceramic salamander. We do this because it is impressive, my wife loves it, it is nearly our wedding anniversary and I am too faint to argue. It is admittedly my fault for alerting her to its charms. Had I not done so I believe she would have passed by without noticing it hanging high up on the wall but I felt obliged to draw her attention to it. "It grieves me to say so," I said, "But I think you ought to see this; he's really rather fine." Of such foolishness is exhaustion the culprit.

At the airport we stagger up to the check-in desk where we are greeted by the amiable Shacoy. The case (now full) presents no problem. I put the flat-packed teak table, copiously wrapped, on the scales.

"What's that?" he says.

"A table."

"What?"

"A TABLE, A FLAT-PACKED TABLE."

Smile, "Is it fragile?"

"Yes" (not really). Then comes the salamander.

"And what's this?" demands our friendly check-in steward. Swathed in bubble wrap with its bright Inca coloured tail sticking jauntily out of one end of the packing it looks like a badly mummified Egyptian pharaoh.

"It's a lizard."

"A what?!"

"A lizard . . ."

Smile, "Say again?"

". . . a CERAMIC LIZARD."

"Er . . . . I see." Sending us on our way he beckons the next passengers forward with unconcealed relief.

Large G and Ts are in order in the departure lounge to postpone incipient mental collapse. These arrive just in time for a Bahamasair announcement that there will be a half hour delay because they "are replacing a few light bulbs on the aircraft"—It is broad daylight for heaven's sake! 45 minutes late we board and try to fit the salamander on our laps without gouging out the eyes or filling other orifices of our fellow returning passengers who seem to have got even bigger since the flight out this morning. Nonetheless, the flight leaves without faltering and we return to Exuma, supper and bed quite exhausted by this thrilling excursion but immensely proud to have achieved this Da-Glo reptilian icon squatting on our dining table.

ooooooooOooooooooo

I need to pay our electricity bill at the offices of the Bahamas Electricity Company known locally as BEC; always a good idea so that one gets a receipt and can talk to the cashier if any hiccoughs arise as they not infrequently do. Clad in the usual tee shirt, shorts and flip-flops I sit down to wait my turn; a similarly dressed friend who is Bahamian arrives and joins me. After a short pause he ponders, "Where else but Exuma would you go and sit in the electricity board's offices to pay your bill with your feet covered in sand?" And I look down at our feet . . . . it is true!

ooooooooOooooooooo

It is Tuesday which means that the supply boat from Nassau is due. So, this morning I am going to the boat to collect two sacks of dog meal. I reach the dockside at 9.45 and the Grand Master, known colloquially as the "Grand Disaster" is already moored and unloading but the Sea Link ferry, which has my cargo on board, is standing off. After an hour the Grand Master condescends to move over to the second dock to allow the ferry a chance. The ferry approaches the dock stern-on and muffs it. She pulls out to sea to try again with the same result; it is a choppy day. Third time lucky; and she begins to unload. It is now mid morning; the wind that is keeping the whitecaps on the ocean is also keeping the sky a bright and clear blue and the sun is beaming down some serious rays. It is hot.

At this point both fork lift trucks responsible run out of electricity and are obliged to stop while replacement batteries are fitted. Unloading resumes. I still cannot see our dog food sacks as all the pallets are covered with tarpaulins. Finally I spot them right at the back. In the meantime I try to phone L several times to explain the situation but Batelco, the island's telecoms company are obviously having an away day and have cut off supplies to all pay-as-you-go mobiles. (They do this periodically at the behest of Immigration so that any illegal Haitians on the island can be rounded up for deportation secure in the knowledge that those caught cannot mobile their friends and relatives to alert them.) I dare not drive home as I will lose my good parking place and the dock is a zoo. I dare not leave the shipping office in case I lose my place in the queue outside—obtaining the goods is one thing, paying the shipping fees for them is quite another.

One of the forklifts breaks down again and amid much gesticulation yet another battery is obtained and fitted. This fails to do the business so an ear-splitting debate ensues with rich

Bahamian baritones growling at each other in the midst of an ever-growing and excitable crowd. Eventually, yes—eureka! They discover it has run out of fuel. A 5 gallon drum is procured and the truck is resuscitated. I finally get my hands on the dog food at 1.15pm having spent the previous 3 hours living hopefully and trying to stay in the shade. When will I learn to bring a book to read. But the afternoon washes away the frustration. We take a picnic and, having anchored our boat in a little sandy bay, go for a pre-lunch dip in the warm turquoise waters. As we sit eating, rocking gently in the shadow of the boat's "Bimini", the pcrambulator type canvas shelter that is installed on all boats hereabouts, an urge to snooze becomes too impossible to resist.

CHAPTER 32

Our kind neighbours Frank and Elvira have offered to show me round Richmond Hill one of the island's three "ghost villages". We will go in their car, an ancient Nissan Sunny which they bought when it became superannuated as a hire car. Before they returned to the island this autumn a crazed Haitian burglar broke into the car through a passenger door, ripping out the rear seat back squab in order to access the boot where he stole the tyre jack. (He also broke into the house next door, spent the night and stole some of the owner's clothes on his way out but was quickly apprehended by the constabulary when the owner recognised his t-shirt and trainers being worn by the thief in the local supermarket the following morning). I am to sit in the back seat but am advised to hang on to the passenger seat in front to avoid being catapulted into the boot in the event of an unscheduled stop. This position involves some discomfort and back pain. And, to be blunt, the car is stuffy but my window will only open on direction from the driver. I am unwilling to invoke this activity in case malodorous breezes waft in during the journey and tempt me to defenestrate or require further adjustment by Frank, thereby dangerously distracting him. (I have not been a passenger of Frank's before but he has the aura of the absent-minded professor about him and looks dangerously distractable. He is, after all, an agronomist.)

We embark which takes some little time as Frank is tall and has to concertina his legs into the driver's foot well. A slightly embarrassing silence ensues as Frank begins grovelling around under the dashboard with his head firmly jammed against the steering wheel. Dark mutterings from within elicit the fact that although the ignition key turns freely in the ignition it no longer works and indeed is rusted permanently into place. It transpires that the reason for the breathless search under the dash is to locate the secondary ignition switch which has been fitted to circumvent this problem. Finally the necessary hotwire takes effect and we are ready to go. But Frank has decided that for a journey of this magnitude he had better check the tyres. And unwinds himself accordingly. Sure enough we have a near flat. As we have no jack the solution is to hop, skip and clump for the few miles to the "Blessed Full" filling station where air is to be had. Frank repeats the starting ritual and we are off.

We arrive without incident although my mouth feels full of loosened fillings. Frank uncoils and the quest for air begins. The air hose and nozzle are clearly available and ready for action. The man to start the generator and compressor is not. After some minutes of aggressive encouragement in Bahamian, (actually English but with such a heavy accent as to be unintelligible), from the cashier he appears from the back of the building. The tyre is filled then the cashier is petitioned to release the garage's only tyre pressure gauge from the till so that we may confirm that all four tyres are at approximately the same pressure. The tyres are checked, pronounced adequate and we are off.

As we penetrate further and further into the jungle we suddenly and improbably come across a 750 yard stretch of dual carriageway. It is the only bit on the island and is being swiftly reclaimed by the bush. It seems surreal that this piece of "motorway" should exist anywhere on Exuma let alone here in the middle of absolutely nowhere. It is even too narrow for smugglers' planes to land, the only other possible use for it. As its sole destination is Richmond Hill one can only pause to consider what must have been in the minds of the highways and planning people when this Quixotic gesture was fomented.

Richmond Hill is a deserted village at the north-west end of the island. Once it was a farming community, one of the "bread baskets" of Exuma, supplying fruit and vegetables to the populace, but not enough to justify a dual carriageway. Looking carefully at the bush on the way in, one comes suddenly upon Bougainvillaea arching up through the trees and one or two other varieties of domestic shrubs and plants which indicate the hamlet's concealed location. The village, which consisted of some fourteen cottages, supported its own school and a delightful little church. The last occupant, the rector, left about 35 years ago so all is now in ruins. The church although roofless still has its pews and kneelers together with its pulpit in place; doors, windows and shutters are long gone. Even with the sleepy, dappled sunshine falling warmly through the trees the spot has a sadly dilapidated air; one can only speculate as to how vibrant such a community might have been during its flourishing years.

As we begin our tour along overgrown paths I wonder about the chance of poisonwood. Merely standing under it during a rainstorm can lead to painful blisters on all exposed skin. Because the sap is not water soluble it cannot be washed off with soap and water and spreads when the lesions are, inevitably, scratched. The toxins attack the body's immune systems and often the only effective way to get rid of it is by hospitalisation and massive doses of prednisalone—a local remedy is to spray the affected parts with WD40 which dissolves the sap and does goodness knows what else. When the tree trunk is hit the bleeding sap creates black spots on its reddish bark which makes the adult tree fairly easily recognisable. Unfortunately the young saplings are another matter as this marking is not present on them. After encountering some strange looking shrubs I say to Frank, who is an agronomist after all, (what exactly is an agronomist?) "Do you know what poisonwood looks like?" "No, do you?" he responds. We both ponder this in thoughtful silence. But our further explorations and return to George Town are uneventful.

Frank and Elvira's car has since gone to the great car park in the sky and has been replaced by a newly retired rental car. Given the spectacular character of the previous machine we await this one's progress with keen anticipation. As a post script the new machine is a great disappointment; it is quite capable of comparative swiftness as is witnessed by the fact that they incur two speeding tickets during the evening on successive weekends. I harbour dark suspicions that one of these evenings was the occasion when, as related to me by Elvira, she and Frank, whilst at Eddie's Edgewater for Rake and Scrape, witnessed two "very louche young ladies behaving in a disgraceful manner, in fact they were 'pole dancing'!" This sounds terribly risqué not to say implausible for George Town, so I am intrigued to know what the girls were really doing; if Eddie's <u>had</u> a pole they'd limbo it.

ooooooooOooooooooo

For a number of years Elvira has organised the Exuma Gardening Club and, hence, the annual Horticultural Show both of which have been highly successful to her great credit and undeniable efforts. On one occasion a rather deaf friend involved in the Show rang up to ask for her telephone number "You know, that woman who's your neighbour, what's her name . . . El Virus?" We are so impressed; we couldn't have dreamt up this nickname in a hundred years. She is undoubtedly Exuma's answer to Che Guevara or was she the baddy in "The Magnificent Seven"?

CHAPTER 33

And so to the Bahamas Water and Sewerage Company offices to pay our quarterly bill which we have not yet received. As with all public services here they will cut off your supply irrespective of whether they have sent you a bill, or not. I am standing behind a large well-endowed Bahamian woman at the counter: she is conducting a conversation with the attractive woman, "of traditional build" as author Alexander McCall Smith would call it, who is sitting at a desk some distance away at the rear of the office filling in a mail order form from a catalogue.

"What did you say you wanted, a G-STRING?"

"Yes."

"What colour?"

"Pink."

"Sick?!"

"PINK!"

"OK, no problem, man." I am obliged to view the lady with renewed interest, having not appreciated that such lubricious discussion was the daily fare of the Water Company's staff.

ooooooooOoooooooo

It is Christmas Eve and we have invited some friends in for drinks. These are not cocktails as the locals know them which, given that spirits are duty free, means a half pint plastic beaker filled with ice and spirits of your choice with a dash of mixer in the top. One of these renders you wobbly-legged and liable to vertigo; two induces temporary amnesia. We are serving 'Champagne cocktails' a deceptively innocuous blend of sparkling wine, sugar and brandy. Our guests arrive at six and the idea is to shoo them out at seven thirty so that we can go to the airport and collect our daughter off the last flight before Christmas. She has been to a wedding in India and it will take her 30 hours to travel from Delhi to Milan to Miami to Exuma. She is renowned within the family for being able, single-handedly, to double the official time taken by any mode of transport so we are not optimistic about her chances of arriving pre-Christmas. L rings the airport at seven to be assured that the flight will come in ten minutes early! We hurriedly leave our party and dash to collect her. When we return the party is not only still in full swing but additional guests, relatives of those invited, have materialised. But 'tis the season of goodwill and all are welcome. Some time later the revellers totter off into the night; many have been beguiled by the misleadingly bland and fruity taste of the brandy cocktails, especially our American friends who have not come across them before and treat them with some misplaced levity and not a little disrespect. "Is this alcoholic?" goes the refrain. Brits who have had them before merely ignore the potential outcome on grounds of celebration. Witness our friend Alexander discoursing subsequently on the party where he had had a number of the cocktails. "Lovely party; thanks awfully for driving us home!" (We didn't.)

oooooooo0ooooooooo

After a fortnight of iffy weather Christmas Day dawns warm, sunny with a clear blue sky, and brisk wind. We rush to pack for a boat trip. This involves major logistics. Beach towels for everyone including the dog: dog's bowl, dog's water, dog's lead, dog's parasol, our parasol, half a gallon of drinking water, plastic wine glasses, bottle of wine, plastic box containing "banana" sandwiches (that is, they are encased in clingfilm so that they can be peeled then re-sealed to avoid sand sticking to the fillings—someone always wants something urgently or the dog starts digging a hole just as you have started your sandwich—Sod's Law applies.) Also packed in the bag are anoraks (in case of a sudden tropical shower), sun creams of assorted factors, boat keys, two way radio, money, paperbacks, mobile phone, sun specs, reading specs together with sundry other wifely and daughterly essentials. All is put into the car along with the dog and the humans for the short (just as well) drive to the boatyard. We travel across Elizabeth Harbour enduring tossing whitecaps and a fair wetting. Finding that the bay next to our usual one is the more sheltered of the two we drop anchor and unload. First job is to retrieve a coconut from our store in the boat console and throw it hard shore-wards. This is the signal for the dog to hurl himself into the turquoise shallows after it which means that, with him distracted, we can unload the boat in relatively dry conditions. An excited, cavorting German Shepherd can make a lot of spray! And our baggage is damp enough as it is. We set up camp on beautiful coral sand; ours, as usual, are the first and only footprints on the beach. It is interesting to note that unlike the shell sand of the Mediterranean our coral sand never becomes unbearably hot, just luxuriously warm. Sunbathing, swimming and general indolence are in order to revive our weary global traveller from her circumnavigation. Christmas lunch takes the form of smoked salmon sandwiches and champagne; dress is the usual Bahamian format for such occasions—swimming gear. Afterwards a snooze is unavoidable as we drop off to the sound of wavelets three feet from us and the gentle soughing of a warm caressing breeze through the thatch palms ringing the cove behind.

CHAPTER 34

Yesterday we presented ourselves at the Immigration Office (a tiny cubicle in the Administration Building) to renew our visas, as instructed. L has been off island recently so has plenty of time left. My visa, on the other hand, expired today and the immigration officer having misled L into thinking he would simply renew it announced that the only way this could be done would be for me to leave the country and return, what the Americans who seem to have experience of these matters call "going round the flag". So today I fly to Miami on the 8.15am flight, hopefully to return at lunchtime assuming that I can get a standby seat; a total waste of half a day and $300. Failing this it will be the evening flight with a whole day in Miami airport.

However, flying out early in the morning over the Exuma cays has its compensations. Looking down, the colours are spectacular as the small island jewels pass under us in settings of coral sand and turquoise shallows with tiny white dots of yachts moored up like charms on bracelets. We are passing through trade wind cotton wool balls of cloud and below is God's palette of every conceivable variation of blue from palest duck egg through to deepest ultramarine. The sea bed has been shaped by the currents to a subterranean desert with sand dunes, ridges and valleys.

Miami is a very flat city. Not only is it very low-lying, it is also superimposed on a latticework of canals and lakes which look man-made although I suspect that this is because their edges have been straightened and filled to provide appropriate housing plots. Row upon row of little boxes, many with the obligatory bright blue kidney-shaped swimming pool, shine brightly as the plane descends in the early morning sunshine.

I cannot find where to check in but eventually see a small circular American Eagle customer services desk in the middle of the concourse. In desperation I ask the stewardess manning it "Where do I go to check in?" "Here's fine," she states. What a relief. Changing my flight to the midday one is no problem. Looking at her terminal she smiles, "I think we can squeeze you on; would you prefer aisle or window?" "Aisle, please", "What row would you prefer?!" She re-designates my tickets and scrawling four "S"s on it directs me to the boarding gate. On arrival at security the guard eyes my four "S"ed ticket with a predatory gleam, "Step this way would you please sir", he commands leading me to a simulation of a modern telephone kiosk. "I want you to step inside and wait until the green light shows before you come out, OK?" Er . . . what is it?" "It's an Explosive Trace Portal and you will be directed to an exit when the test is complete." I can see no traces of others who have preceded me or indeed evidence of their explosive qualities but cannot decide whether this is good news or bad. I am tempted to air a cheery, "Beam me up Scotty!" but am mindful that we nearly lost our then teenage son in similar circumstances when he muttered "Anyone would think I had a bomb in my pocket,"—and that was in England. I have no wish to break boulders so submit weakly. Nothing happens for some time then, 'Tout a coup' as the French would say the kiosk spits at me from all directions simultaneously. This is pretty unnerving but I am ready the next time. In all there are three explosive spits before the light goes green. I leave feeling normal but mildly insulted (I have never been spat on by a telephone kiosk, even in England), and look for my luggage, a Marks and Spencer plastic supermarket bag with a paperback, a pencil, a note-book, a rubber (eraser for our American cousins) and two tissues, just in case.

I am summarily pounced on by an impossibly tall guard with an equally predatory gleam and rubber gloves. "Oh heavens, it really isn't my day," I think. "Please identify your luggage, sir," in a polite but firm voice; given his size the phrase "no nonsense" comes to mind. I pick up my paltry plastic bag. "Is that all?!" he asks in a disbelieving tone. "'Fraid so," I say apologetically. Perhaps he wants a matching set of five Louis Vuitton suitcases and a white poodle to keep his hand in. Then the penny drops "Hey, this is my lucky day!" He beams, grabs my bag and then another thought occurs "Nothing sharp or dangerous in here is there?" as he peers suspiciously into the bag. "Er, no." Am I unwittingly concealing a nuclear device in my pencil? My imagination has deserted me at this point. He grabs a swab which he probes into the bag, wipes it round thoroughly, presumably for drugs or explosives, and inserts it into a machine which, shortly, burps and flashes a green light. Then he extracts each item with the air of a bomb disposal expert and inspects them minutely. Finally, he gets to the paperback. "Looks like the genuine thing to me," he mutters, riffling through it. Then, with the air of one for whom the tablets have just arrived from the mountain, he looks at me, smiles and says "That's all, you're free to go, sir. Have a nice day." He points vaguely towards a corridor entrance and I stumble into it.

On my return to Exuma I am immediately stopped in the airport terminal for a disagreeable altercation with the duty immigration official. He tells me that I can't come back in after such a short time and I explain that I have done precisely what I was instructed to do to renew my visa by his superior at the office in George Town. Eventually he asks "What status do you have on the island?" "I live here, I have a home here!" I exclaim in exasperation. "Oh, why didn't you say so before?" he grumps, stamping my passport with unconcealed irritation. I leave for the embrace of my wife and a lift home to the sanity of a beautiful tropical view.

ooooooooOoooooooo

Taking friends to the airport recently we are nearly wiped out by a red truck being towed as is starts to overtake the towing vehicle in our lane and then narrowly avoids crashing into a row of palm trees on the verge. The red truck has no tyres and is running on the protesting wheel rims which grind out a cacophonous din where they contact the unyielding tarmac. On our return trip, however, closer inspection reveals that two distinct tramlines have been forged by this automotive scrapheap and the Queens Highway looks like a demolition derby with smouldering old car parts liberally strewn in profusion all the way back. On our way we decide to drop in Norman Wells at The Cays.

Our friend Norman has a road running past his development and a mild obsession about keeping traffic speed down to avoid damage to its surface which he and others have paid for, dearly. His solution is speed bumps or, more accurately, speed Himalayas—one really needs a tracked vehicle to traverse them; a tank comes to mind. One day shortly after these formidable structures have been sunk into the road we watch a wondrous scene unfold. Two Bahamians have come barrelling down the hardcore in an aged saloon, striking the bump at speed and launching the car's front end into the air. Unfortunately the rear is disinclined to follow so the whole vehicle comes down with a resounding crunch—landing squarely on the bump, precariously balanced on the centre of it, all four wheels off the road. Swiftly the chassis cannot take any more whereupon, magnificently, the boot springs open with a loud report like a circus clowns' car—all that is missing is the proverbial backfire. Eventually the Bahamians decide to extract themselves to review the situation and manhandle the car. Amid shouts of "Hey man dat's some bump," they rock it off the offending obstruction to the sounds of tortured metal the better to continue their journey. By now it is looking distinctly droopy around the midriff but miraculously the doors still close and off they go.

CHAPTER 35

We have been back to the UK for our first family Christmas in ten years and have been snowed in for several weeks. In order to return to the Bahamas we need to break out but our rear wheel drive Volvo is not capable in these conditions. Luckily our dear friend Val arranges to collect us in her farm 4 wheel drive truck so we jump aboard for the trip south to Newcastle airport. Our luggage lies in the rear, like a scene from the nativity, nestling on a bed of straw, tufts of which stick out of the tailgate in all directions. The journey through persistent snow showers takes twice as long as expected but we have left at 1pm for a 7.45pm flight to London and so are in plenty of time.

Check-in is no problem and we sit reading in departures watching the snow falling, coating the airport verges and aprons. As planes begin to be delayed we repair to the desk to see if we can buy an upgrade to an earlier flight. No luck, a truculent official tells us we are not allowed to transfer tickets on the day of the flight. The earliest flight leaves half full and we watch it from departures where, as we later discover, the loudspeaker system is not working. Eventually we overhear someone saying passengers on our flight need to report to the ticket desk and collect our luggage from arrivals—the flight has been cancelled.

They say we can go on the 6am flight next morning but our connection from Heathrow is too tight and we could catch the last train for London leaving Newcastle Central station at 8.35pm. This train is still running and mercifully is still on time—hurrah for the good old railway! We board coach G with all our hand luggage and two vast, leaden wheelie suitcases which are extending my arms like rubber bands. We find seats and look around. The coach is a scene from Middle Europe. All around us are the sallow faced armies of Genghis Khan, the men with thick stubble or beards and the women all dark haired and sultry. The coach is noisy with their conversation which is unintelligible and they eye us belligerently. Beneath the babble I begin to sense how a stiletto blade between the lower ribs might feel and wonder how long it takes a mob to reach "murderous"; God willing the train will take four hours. L who presumably has assessed our fellow passengers as thieves and villains decides that as we cannot watch our cases from our seats we should move carriages and goes off on a scouting trip. I and the cases are left alone with the Steppe tribes. She returns after some time saying in a cheerfully loud, inflammatory voice, "I've found this lovely coach which is almost empty and beautifully quiet" "Where is it?" I ask with some reserve. She gives me one of those looks which says "It's on the train, silly!" and replies, "Coach B; I'll take the hand luggage" and sweeps off. I utter a small prayer of thanks for wheelie cases and move to the end of the coach to start the great migration. I then discover that the cases are too wide to travel down the gangway on the wheels by which time L has returned for a second trip and says, brightly, "We'll reach Durham in a minute. When we get there you just get off with the cases and wheel them down the platform to coach B." This has the ring of plausibility about it so I wait, cases poised, by the door for the next stop. As we approach, the guard, or perhaps he is 'customer services director' nowadays, announces lugubriously in a thick Scottish brogue, "Please be exceptionally careful on alighting as the running boards (how quaint!) will be very icy and so will the platform."

As the train halts I leap off, gingerly extracting the two wheelies. The running board is indeed slippery and there is a frighteningly large, dark gap between it and the platform. Raising my eyes I see that the platform, stretching endlessly away, is a heavy piste of snow. In one of those inspirational flashes one gets I understand the loneliness of the long distance runner. I have just taken the handles of both cases to begin this race when, to my horror, the guard blows the whistle and starts slamming doors. Like a Dervish I whirl the wheelies back into coach G thrusting myself in after as the door crashes shut behind me. I am recovering slowly when L reappears, "Ah! Here you are," she says as though addressing a truant schoolboy. Through exhausted lips I murmur, "I'll have to drag the cases down." And proceed. By now the Mongolian hoards have fallen into a stupor so the gangway is a tangle of heads, arms, elbows, legs and feet. I stumble through with a rictus grin apologising as I crack heads, swipe elbows and tread on feet leaving behind mutinous stares from dark, murderous hooded eyes beneath beetle brows. Eventually I reach coach B with the first wheelie. I then go back for the second one and repeat the process again. Unfortunately, the Eastern hordes have all returned to slumber so once again I stumble along ricocheting from side to side cracking elbows and feet in profusion. By this time I have a slight sense of humour failure and the apology bucket is empty. Vile remarks and curses flow copiously in languages thankfully unknown to me while the term 'lynch mob' darts in and out of my overheated mind. Finally all is safely installed in coach B and as I collapse into my seat, a broken man, L says brightly, "I could just do with a good drink now." I receive this news with some hesitation—the idea is a good one but the buffet car is well beyond coach G . . . .

The train duly arrives at Kings Cross station at 12.30am where we learn that the tube will not run out to the airport and that the mainline Heathrow Express is finished for the night. We are accosted on the concourse by a gentleman from one of our former colonies "Very good taxis, very, very good taxis, very good prices." We decline khaki cornucopia and move to the official rank, which is empty. After 20 minutes in the snow a black cab arrives, "Heathrow? That'll be 60 quid guv". As we are standing with some Canadians we have met escaping from Newcastle and in a similar predicament to ours we decide to share. This proves to be a mixed blessing, not only are we well over-baggaged but so are the Canadians. And on further inspection the male of the couple is built like a moose. We decide to put the women and luggage in first, particularly as the cabbie is getting cold feet (no pun intended). I then persuade the moose to disassemble himself into convenient lengths so that he might fit his limbs and torso into the shrinking cab space. This he does and his knees now appear to be stuffed up his nostrils. I dance lightly into the remaining spaces putting one leg to his right and my other knee intimately in his groin. We smile weakly at each other, commencing a mildly forced discussion of world affairs. At the first destination the cab drops the Canadians before us so the whole process has to be reversed, which causes some problems as, by now, everyone has been coiled up in a ball of string tangle of limbs and luggage for 50 minutes. Released onto the pavement we all stagger about like drunks as our bodies unwind themselves, portions of arms and legs jerking uncontrollably like bits of old bedsprings. The eventual fare is £80 but the Canadians with great foresight have left £40 which is OK.

We reach our hotel in terminal 5 at 2am to be greatly disappointed. L has booked a good room because we thought we would have the whole evening and a lazy morning and they had upgraded us to an even better room. However, we are too tired to do anything but fall into bed except, that is, for sustenance. We have not eaten since lunch time so decide looking at the room service menu that bowls of lentil soup sound just right. I ring to order and a prim voice announces that as the menu soup entry does not sport a diamond icon beside it, it is only available in the restaurant, which is closed. There is nothing vaguely inspiring with the diamond (is this a conspiracy?) and so to bed.

In the morning the snow has followed us down the country bogging things down as it comes. It suddenly seems like a good idea to leave the hotel and go to the terminal very swiftly in case of delays, queues etc. We can catch breakfast there once we have checked in. At the terminal we join a queue of epic proportions whose tail is just inside the terminal door. This is Virgin's "Fast Bag Drop"! 2.5 hours later we reach the counter; the clock is ticking. As one case is 5 lbs overweight we can either buy another bag, repack and rejoin the queue or pay £30 excess baggage charge. We are fed up and do this. Then my hand luggage is spotted and the officious check-in woman insists that it be weighed as well. The limit for this is apparently 5.5lbs and mine is 16lbs. Some of this will have to go as hold luggage. Luckily L has a carrier bag secreted about her person so the laptop and vital documents go in this. My hand luggage is consigned to the aircraft's belly. The carrier bag weighs 12lbs but the officious woman seems unworried about this. Next we have to join another queue to pay for our excess baggage. We plead our way forward as time is running out. Finally we reach the departure lounge in time for the flight to be called. Not time for breakfast now—anyway it is now 12 .30 and we left the hotel at 8am. We board the aircraft which sits on the apron for 1.5 hours while ever heavier snow falls and spray machines de-ice the wings. "Anyone would think this was Canada for heavens sake" I opine to L. At last, to our infinite relief, we take off for Miami.

The following day we see that 52 flights out of Heathrow were cancelled because of bad weather. And the airport eventually closed.

Small things matter. Few moments are as heartwarming as a booming "Welcome home!" from a beaming immigration lady at Nassau Airport: the greeting because she has spotted the entry stamps in our passports from arrivals on previous occasions. This event can also be sometimes mildly embarrassing when the official has spent time in Exuma and sees us languishing back down the queue. "HEY MR AND MRS HESLOP, COME HERE, COME HERE!" she yells as we sheepishly disengage from the crowd and queue-jump a bunch of hot and by now smouldering tourists for a convivial conversation at the immigration desk about her time on the island, we whispering uncomfortably and she shouting with pleasure.

CHAPTER 36

The other night we were taken out to January Cay restaurant by our house guests. We took our own wine, paying the corkage because buying this restaurant's wine needs a bank loan and were regaled by the ebullient owner with a high-powered sales pitch while we tried to choose our meals from the menu. If the owner was over the top, the food was good. I had conch chowder which was dark and spicy followed by roast breast of chicken supreme with sweet pea risotto—emphatically not Bahamian food which made a nice change—and the accompanying risotto came, strangely, in a small coffee cup complete with handle. Although we were sitting inside their canvas awning out of the wind we were able to look out on the little marina as the boats swung beside the mooring jetties all lit up, as was the water, by spotlights above and below the water-level. It is a very attractive setting.

As the evening wore on I was subjected to a monologue of 'business management speak' by our male guest and fell into a gloom. (I retired to escape this sort of nonsense!) However, the evening took a sharp turn for the better when the chef decided to close the kitchen for the night. I heard the door bang and it was as though he had said "Everybody out!" Listening to the business lecture with half an ear I caught, fleetingly from the corner of my eye, a dark brown creature about the size of a small tin lid dash past with spindly legs twinkling and long antennae twitching, then another and then another. At this point I debated revealing this to our female diners but decided to maintain a discrete silence hoping for the impact of surprise. To my delight, acknowledgement was not long in coming; immediately L spotted them and, energised, let out an "Arrrrgh! Cockroaches!" whipping her feet off the floor, whereupon our female guest saw them, too "Oh my God!" bringing her legs smartly up to table height, too. By this time they were darting everywhere, a regular plague of the blighters and real whoppers too. Tearing around all over the floor and leaping from the soffits and curtains, the place was crawling with them. I couldn't restrain an enormous grin, "Well now, great stuff, what a floor show! Any one would think that the Pied Piper had just walked through. Just as well we'd finished supper!" I enthused. And then they disappeared as fast as they had arrived.

As we left L sauntered over to the restaurant owner who was entertaining at the next table and whispered archly "I think you may have an interesting cockroach problem; most of your diners are freeloading!" He gave her a wary, imperceptible nod. But what entertainment, what a performance! It seemed just like a horror film—Alfred Hitchcock's "Invasion of the cockroaches". What a magnificent circus to end the evening! Beat any management seminar I've ever been to into a cocked hat.

oooooooo0ooooooooo

Normal dress for these climes on rising is to throw on a tee shirt, shorts and flip-flops. Is it the lack of constricting clothes, freedom of limbs, the beguiling warmth or a combination of all these that makes people feel sexy and want to cast off their inhibitions with their (few) clothes at any opportunity? I can't say. In any event, despite it being illegal in the Bahamas, we have "surprised" a number of nude bathers on our beach walks with the dog over time—strangers and folks we have known. The syndrome seems to affect them regardless and may have something to do with the fact that there just seems to be a lot of it about. The other day we watched a couple of copulating boa constrictors in the garden oblivious to the tropical rain shower that was cascading down on them. The foreplay was all very sinuous, languorous and lubricious as they twined themselves around each other in the mating dance. Afterwards they slid off into the undergrowth going their separate ways.

Whatever the reasons for feeling good, there is no doubt that the tropical humidity is such that whenever we leave the island our faces seem to shrivel up on our return to the UK. Coming the other way though, they seem to rehydrate and 'plump up," the lines disappearing within days and one seems to feel younger; UK worries and cares manage to melt away as one falls under the spell of this tropical paradise island in the sun.

An alternative plan seems to be to organise a visit to the States where the good burghers of Sarasota are profiting. At least it would appear so to judge from the steady stream of friends and acquaintances who make the pilgrimage for a few weeks "break from the island." Mysteriously they return wrinkle free and looking indefinably younger, if slightly pink about the gills for a month or so.

On this subject our friend and neighbour Bill drops in having just got back from the States where, unbeknown to us, he has undergone a laser face peel under local anaesthetic. The treatment takes precisely 4.47 seconds which says a great deal about the precision needed to avoid a burn-up. The peel subjected him to extreme pain for a whole week following the procedure. After some preliminary chitchat he says with evident pride, "Well, do I look different?" L gives him a quizzical look and cocks her head to one side "I know," she beams, "You've had your hair cut and trimmed your beard!" Er . . . . not quite!

Coming clean, Bill then proceeds to tell us a horror story of what was involved in this beautification process which included taking copious pain-killers and walking around all day with ice packs held to his face to try and reduce the raw ache.

ooooooooOooooooooo

Here we go again! Our one and only newly opened coffee shop the Driftwood Café is having a soirée to raise awareness even though it is opposite the Peace and Plenty in the centre of town. So, by way of support our party, consisting of Andy and Debbie, is going along for dinner which will be al fresco in the warm Bahamian night.

We are seated at one end of a long table lit by flickering candles. The party sharing with us at the other end includes our neighbours Kent Polly the boss of Minns Watersports boatyard and his wife the long-legged Diane who owns and runs our little Caribbean treasure chest of a gift shop "Sandpiper," her sister and husband and other merrymakers.

Much earlier in the day, before breakfast, I used the short-cut path past her garden to go up to Bill's house for some keys and aroused the ire of her dog Skeeter (short for mosquito) who voiced his ire in a dissonance of howls, yelps, barks and growls.

Spying me down the table Diane yells coquettishly "Hey Mike, was that you passing my yard this morning? Next time you do that can you ring me? 'Cos when Skeeter barks I come running out to see what's up and sometimes I don't sleep with much on." I explain to her party, "Naturally, I'll now do this deliberately!—because I know I only have to irritate Skeeter and out comes the scantily clad Diane!" I do believe that beneath her suntan, Diane is blushing becomingly.

oooooooo0oooooooo

Our new(ish) next door neighbour Steven, for it is he, has bought a boat. It is an 18 foot Boston Whaler lookalike with chrome rails on the bow and smoked glass screens on the driver and passenger consoles, altogether quite a slick machine. He is one of the breed that believes "There is nothing to driving a boat;" he is one of the "its just like a car, point it and go" brigade and chooses Easter Sunday for its maiden voyage, bringing it round to the house during the morning with some strong south east winds and a fair degree of chop. The neighbourhood is quiet and the locals blissfully unaware of the drama about to be played out. We are, in fact, on a long-distance call to our son in Corfu when a noise like a back hoe tap dancing on a corrugated tin roof interrupts the peace. I leap to my feet, "It must be those damned Uruguyans back to finish Steven's swimming pool" I yell above the racket as I race to the window and peer out. But no, an extraordinary sight is revealing itself. The boat has its outboard motor tilted clear of the water so that each blade of the propeller is just shaving the surface as it sweeps round. The boat itself is describing wild dizzying circles like a dog wanting a walk, bucking to and fro as Miriam (Steven's wife), up to her armpits in water, tries to hold it unsuccessfully and is caught up in a demented embrace, hurtling round with it. Meanwhile Steven in his panama hat is lurching from bow to control console to motor like a mad drunk dancing a fantasy hornpipe—legs and arms flailing insanely as the boat jolts around emitting clouds of acrid blue smoke. I must admit to watching with fascination and some small amusement: Steven is not a chap who invites advice and is clearly a novice skipper.

Having said that we all started from zero at some stage and one still makes mistakes.

As we watch, neighbour Diane goes down to offer assistance but Steven, who among his many talents is also an accomplished chauvinist, sees her coming and gives up the battle at this point, dropping the motor to half tilt thereby destabilising it and so shoots out across the bay in great erratic porpoise swoops and lunging dives like an amusement park rodeo ride.

Diane later says that Bill, who was also watching the whole episode through his binoculars from his hilltop eyrie, felt obliged to take two resuscitative Tylenol tablets to avoid having a coronary. The boat has not ventured back since, so one assumes that Steven is now confining this mayhem to the privacy, or should it be piracy, of the high seas with Miriam's firm blessing; she is not one to suffer fools gladly, particularly in public.

The "Sporage" at rest

CHAPTER 37

The old lady who swallowed the fly has nothing on us. When we first arrived on the island to find land to build on we bought a second hand 'guaranteed' Mitsubishi Pajero from a "friend". We asked him to look after it for us while we were off the island and run it occasionally to keep it ticking over. On our return four months later we discovered that he had been using it to transport building materials, managing to cover about 2600 kilometres in the time—going some on an island only 90 miles long. It never worked properly after that and became so unreliable that we acquired a little Kia Sportage (the t in the name is missing hence its uniquely Scottish nickname the "Sporage" a wondrous sort of Gaelic mélange of sporran and porridge) as back-up so that we could take the dog to the beach and get the shopping. Unfortunately, the Sporage proved to be too small to accommodate guests arriving at the airport to stay with all their luggage.

So we bought the "Oddity" (a Honda Odyssey). Like the others, this is an 'island' car: we bought it for a fair price on its retirement from Keith Thompson Car Hire, that thoroughbred stable for island cars. Keith, who is the brother-in-law of Percy Fox, our favourite realtor (everyone is related), swears by them as being long legged and rugged. Certainly they stand up to treatment by American tourists ranging from occasional forays on the wrong side of the road by way of provoking the rest of us, to full-on off-road safaris through the bush. Ours has several long scrapes down its flanks that might have been animal but are almost certainly vegetable as evidence of these rites of passage. However, we have no complaints; for it has served us valiantly. The march of time has treated the old girl kindly but we finally had to do something about the sunroof which had evolved into a shallow rust pit in the roof where birds bathed after rain. Even when shut, on a good day sunlight did, indeed, filter through it attractively. Keith suggests that I ring an acquaintance of his in Rolleville who wants $500 to block it up. This seems a lot so we decide to go out for competitive tender.

The obvious alternative is Auto Extreme, which is one of the few garages on the island and is close by. It is owned and run by Andrew Parotti, an amiable but daunting man-mountain. L says that at 6ft I look like a child beside him. (I feel like one, too). When his hair is occasionally allowed to burst forth upon his scalp it looks like light brown wire wool. His chin usually sports 2 days (or is it 2 hours) of stubble which looks as though iron stakes have been sunk in his jaw to prevent an invasion beach landing. Back in the UK a comic called the "Dandy" featured a magnificent cartoon wild west character called 'Desperate Dan' who was one of life's natural size XXLs and obligatory reading for all small boys. Today there is even a statue of him in the centre of Dundee, the home of his publishers. Desperate Dan had to shave with a blowtorch and ate enormous "cow pie" with signature pairs of horns sticking out of the pastry crust.

As instructed, I return with the car at noon and enter Andrew's office to find him hunched menacingly over the biggest pizza I have ever seen. I ask diffidently whether he'd like to look at the Oddity's roof. He grunts and ambles prehistorically out of the office, registering on the Richter Scale. He places an ursine finger the size of a belaying pin lovingly on the rust, "How pretty do you want it?" He chuckles a Jolly Green Giant sort of chuckle: "I don't give a . . . ." I smile timidly. "I can do it for $150". A deal is struck. In due course the Oddity is released: it now has a roof section where the weather was that is not so much a body panel as armour plate. If the need ever arises we can confidently mount some form of heavy calibre automatic weapon on it.

As I drive it back and accelerate to 35miles per hour I spy a small yellow and green lizard hanging onto the windscreen wiper for dear life. I slow down to a more gentle speed and he manages to retain his passenger status until we reach home. On arrival I open the car door slowly the better to inspect him; the poor little fellow is so traumatised that he hops onto my hand for a moment before jumping onto the oleanders beside the porch stairs and disappearing gratefully into the foliage.

ooooooooOooooooooo

Not for nothing is Andrew's garage named Auto Extreme: it lives up to its name on a daily basis. Recently, the Sporage seemed to be pulling to the right when the brakes were applied. This is alarming at the best of times but given that it is left hand drive on roads which drive on the left it puts the passenger (me) who is sitting in the suicide seat, in the centre of the road, on a direct collision course with oncoming traffic as we swerve towards it with seemingly magnetic verve. A trip to what might reasonably be abbreviated to A & E produces the diagnosis from Andrew that we need a new brake calliper.

The Sporage is left in tender care and duly collected when fixed. As there seems to be little improvement a second 'black market' view is sought. It turns out that the nearside brake has been 'fixed' by severing the brake pipe, stuffing a nail up the resulting hole in the end and crimping it with pliers to seal it off. With only the right-hand brake working driving has become an art of balancing it against a contra turn on the steering wheel to achieve anything approaching a straight course—definitely not recommended on a Friday evening when approaching the customary weekend police 'traffic and drink' check. This said, one has immense sympathy for Auto Extreme's philosophy which is that bearing in mind the eye-watering cost of bringing cars and parts into the Bahamas it tries really hard, doing everything it can to keep its customers' cars running at minimal cost and inconvenience, even if the message gets a bit muddled sometimes.

Recently, the Honda's wheel-wobble has evolved to the point where steering is pretty much a lottery. I book it in for a check-up. "Just bring it in for 8.30 tomorrow," Andrew says. Mid-afternoon the following day I ring to enquire tenderly after progress and am told that the car requires two new tyres. "How can this be?" I howl, "There must be some mistake, there's masses of tread on them, you cannot be serious." I may not be a petrol head but I do feel competent to discuss tyres with assurance, for Heaven's sake. "It need two new tyres, sir." "But what's wrong with them?" "De tyres are lumpy." I am unfamiliar with this fault; clearly, I am out of my depth. "OK," I mutter.

ooooooooOoooooooo

The white heat of automotive revolution is upon us: the Exuma office of the Department of Public Works is installing cats' eyes down the centre (mostly) of the Queen's Highway from George Town north. This improvement has increased traffic speeds as affirmed by the sound of racing engines; indeed, as the road runs parallel to the airport it is hard to tell whether planes are trying to land on it or cars take off. At least the cats' eyes clearly show the general direction of the road so that when entering bends the natives are encouraged to adjust, marginally, the steering wheel. This should reduce accidents and deter the locals from attempting to drive round curves in straight lines ending in close encounters with the bush.

CHAPTER 38

As time passes so one gets used to the words and phrases that the Exumans use which have their own unique meaning. When one wants to see the bank manager or anyone else in a position of bureaucratic authority one is invariably met with the phrase, "He just stepped out" which can mean anything from he isn't in yet, he's gone to the loo, or having a chat, or is out for a long lunch, to he's gone home early. More permanently, if an islander says "Elvis he late," (Elvis is quite a popular name hereabouts) it doesn't just mean he's behind schedule—it means he's dead! Frequently when asking a question the verb will be placed at the end of the sentence as in "Who dat is?" for "Who is that?" and someone's arrival will be described thus, "He done reach". When a request is made of someone for information, often as not, it will be retold "I 'axed' him for his view." Occasionally, when one is suffering from a frustrating interlude trying to ascertain when something will happen the placatory phrase "Soon come" will be used. This means exactly the opposite for it merely expresses a wish on behalf of the speaker to make your life more bearable, although in the Bahamian time frame it actually represents a strange form of the truth.

One of Exuma's worthies sadly died the other day and preparations were being made for the main event. I was in CNK

Liquor Store on the day before the funeral queuing to pay for booze but couldn't help overhearing the conversation at the counter in front. One Bahamian matron to another, "Are you going to de funeral?" "Oh yes, man." First lady, in foghorn tones, "ARE YOU GOING TO VIEW DE BODY?" "AH DON'T DO BODIES . . . . BUT IT WOULD BE NICE TO SEE HOW HE'S LAID OUT."

I heard an apocryphal but instructive story recently. A Spanish tourist in the Peace and Plenty bar asks the Bahamian barman, "En Espagna we have a saying "mañana"—do you have a word in the Bahamas with the same meaning?" The barman responds, "No man, we have no similar word in de Bahamas which expresses such a powerful sense of urgency."

ooooooooOoooooooo

When it rains here the rain is very wet and its cold! This is a constant surprise to me, my meteorology being unsophisticated at best, not to say decidedly dodgy, although it seems logical if I think about it as the atmosphere is pretty cool higher up. Initially, we could not understand why islanders would refuse to come to work if rain was in the offing but we learnt by experience.

Anyway, we have been advised that if we are caught out in the boat in a tropical shower the best thing to do is put clothes, towels etc into the storage lockers to keep dry and jump into the water which, of course, is warm. (One can get too cocky about this and completely misjudge the speed with which the clouds can form and a shower spring up.) When the inevitable happens, this we do. Immersed in the ocean, we and daughter Sophie squat up to our necks in it sheltering under her plastic sunbathing lilo. Here we sit like the three wise(?) monkeys completely sodden, hair in rats-tails, as the rain beats a tattoo on the lilo above and cascades off every conceivable surface. The strength of the downpour makes the sea boil and renders even the shore only some fifteen yards away almost invisible. As we peer out from underneath our refuge and appreciate our circumstances the ridiculousness of it all hits us and we are reduced to helpless laughter. "Well, I suppose I couldn't do this in England," muses Sophie amongst some other choice but less repeatable comments. Shortly, the sun comes out again and we sail on steaming as its rays dry us and the boat off. At one point even the sea is steaming just like wet tarmac on a road after rain; a strange sight, indeed. Sophie decides to swim off the boat and on returning hauls herself out by grabbing the fairing of the tilted engine which the sun has been working on. "Ow! That's jolly hot!" She exclaims. Showers are transitory and soon forgotten, particularly as we are accompanied on our return by the island's playful dolphin pod.

ooooooooOoooooooo

We have a new Batelco (telephone company) senior manager for the island who we are thrilled to discover rejoices in the name of Rolle: we swiftly append the nickname "sausage" with ill-contained glee.

Out here internet is a key service. And ours has been woefully ponderous not to say fitful on occasion. We have spent days, running to months in total, staying in, waiting for Batelco to come and fix the problem and they never turn up on the appointed day. One evening we are muttering darkly about this to our chum Simon who poses a solution. "What you need is a WIMAX box" he says, "It's a WIFI system that takes the signal straight from the tower in George Town and avoids all the dodgy cables and connection crap." This sounds like a sterling idea so L goes off to remonstrate with Sausage and it is agreed.

At our end the system takes the form of a receiving box which goes on the roof. We wait emotionally for the kit to be installed and a fortnight later the engineer appears. We greet him warmly for he has a large cardboard box under his arm which he assures us contains the kit: all is going swimmingly, if slightly leisurely, in the time honoured island manner. We encourage him to make a start and he says affably, "Where do you want it?" "Well, er . . . . we thought up on the roof ridge?" I respond, resisting an impulse to call his wits into question—I always believe in encouraging the troops and think this would be a bad way to start off the job.

"OK, so where's de pole?" He says loftily.

"Er . . . . what pole would that be?"

"You need a 2.5 foot galvanised metal pole attached to the right position on the roof to carry the box," he informs us with evident pleasure.

"Are you sure? Nobody told us about this. So presumably someone else from Batelco has to come and fit the pole?" With sinking heart.

"No sir! We don't do that."

"So we have to get someone else in to do that?" Here we go again.

"Yessir."

"So do we let you know when the pole has been fitted so that you can instal the system?", I retort with just-restrained fury.

"Yessir," he responds enthusiastically as we liberate his container and shuffle him out of the house before murder is committed. We ring our excellent contractor Wade who duly appears the following day at the appointed time and without fuss fits a neat, smart, section of pole to the roof in the desired place. Further persuasive calls are made to Batelco and the engineer returns three days later in a small van whose interior reveals a pair of diminutive domestic stepladders. We go round and mutually admire the new pole. We then ponder the side of the house, some 18 feet from ground level to the eaves.

"But, how do we get up there?" He says, reflectively.

"Ladders," I say, tersely.

"You got ladders?" He enquires.

"Yes," through gritted teeth. (Why am I supposed to provide Batelco with the equipment necessary to do their job I ask myself.)

"Oh," disappointedly.

"Well, there you are," I say, cheerfully.

"Yeah, but it need the cable," he rejoins.

"OK, but presumably that's your department?" I say, cautiously.

"Oh, I can give you the cable but it need to be laid," he replies with finality.

"You mean I need to get someone else in to lay it?!" My astonishment breaks through like a gas bubble in a mud spring. This fellow is not taking his right to life seriously: does he realise that he is in the hands of a man who may well be about to become certifiably and criminally insane? I look at his neck and my hands twitch.

"Yeah, of course! We haven't got time to lay these days—new instructions, sir." He says contentedly. At this point, in default of throwing some crockery L, who, by devious means, has acquired the helpful Mrs Rolle's personal mobile number, makes a call. No, it seems that the engineer is correct and those are the instructions. The engineer dances off merrily leaving us with a coil of cable lying pointlessly on the floor like one of those dozing snakes in a zoo reptile house. "Call me when you laid it," he chants happily, over his shoulder. Once again Wade comes to the rescue laying the cable on the roof, drilling the necessary hole through the wall and feeding it into the house. We advise the engineer and put the ladders out for him: they are locked away, unused, that evening. I haul them out again the next morning—no sign of Batelco. Several days later the engineer appears and commandeers our handyman to 'assist' him, the two of them squatting companionably as a pair of crows on the roof and inexplicably requiring a good half hour of heated dialogue. This is all a mystery: to my knowledge our handyman can just about manage basic plumbing, he has no expertise whatsoever in telephony, still less wireless telephony—what in Heaven's name is he doing up there? Anyway the system is set up. And it works!

A few days later it doesn't. We are back to where we were in the first place except that we are a couple of hundred dollars the poorer for the pole and the cable installation. L calls Mrs Rolle crisply and shortly the engineer pops up. Tests of the line, system and computer prove inconclusive. The engineer is unable to suggest a solution and leaves looking crestfallen. With some asperity L gives all the leads and jackplugs a good hard shove—and hey presto, the system works again! Rather like hitting a recalcitrant island car engine block a good blow with a hammer, occasionally—most efficacious, I find.

Our Batelco engineer calls us on some communications mission and is much exercised by our beautiful purple flowering bougainvillea which climbs up the side of the stairs and stilts as far as the porch verandah. "You need to cut that right back, man—when de day warm up snakes dey climb right up and get in yo house!" A moment of silence follows as we carefully consider him and then the porch. L smiles winningly, "But why wouldn't they just use the stairs like the rest of us?" For the avoidance of doubt this was not Reckly our favourite engineering manager, whom we have nicknamed "direckly" because, whilst charming, he is always late.

CHAPTER 39

The weather forecast for the Bahamas is always good for unintentional entertainment and today proves no exception. "It's going to be very cold tomorrow—could go as low as 19 celsius, so better make the most of it everyone!"

No matter, a new Bahamian restaurant has opened close by under the title "Barbecue Fest". As it is owned by Steve, the good man from the Fish Fry shacks ("Charlie's", to be exact) we are here tonight for supper. The only previous time we have tried it the food took one and a half hours to appear. We had lost the will to live but it was worth the wait. To avoid a repetition of this unfortunate aspect of service I ring at 6.30 to ascertain the contents of the menu and give our order. Sensibly, whilst passing up on a wine list, Steve has declared a corkage charge of $5 per bottle which we think is very reasonable, particularly as Bahamians' ideas of customers' wine preferences can be quite strange and not a little limited.

As a "cold front" is passing through with a howling gale we eschew the table underneath the coconut palm outside in favour of a less climatically challenged spot indoors; mildly disappointing because al fresco eating is one of the pleasures of the Caribbean. But we have learnt by trial and error that ordering a salad upwind of the party is a decorative experience for those downwind. The décor inside is novel. Wallpaper runs down one side of the small room furnished with two tables and a bar at one end. At the other end is a spectacular wallpaper trompe l'oeil featuring a white limestone balustrade and cerulean sea beyond fringed about with palm trees. The good news about the fish and meat is that, unusually, it is all barbecued rather than deep fried. Fried food and diet has created an epidemic of diabetes amongst the Bahamans on the island; the most unusual ingredients have copious sugar added, in particular white bread and coleslaw. L and I both have chosen pork which comes enormous and succulent whilst our chum Bill eats Tilapia, a species of Caribbean fish. All dishes are tasty and come with roast potatoes and salad. Bill has a rum and coke and we drink the bottle of wine we have brought along.

After some time I go to inspect the plumbing—always a dubious expedition in the Bahamas. Inside is a surprise: the actual fittings are rudimentary but work. There are no mosquitoes or other visible bugs to fight off and the lighting is reasonable. Cold running water is complemented by a paper towel roll and a hand soap dispenser. The dispenser contains a highly perfumed substance called "Tropical Garden" coloured a surreal green. It is inert; nothing is swimming in it. It is also well primed and exerting a downward pressure on the plunger releases a horizontal projectile jet straight over the top of the basin like a water cannon at rioters. Lightning reflexes allow me to perform an acrobatic sidestep of Olympian proportions such that the stream spurts past at groin level and reaches the floor in the opposite corner of the room trickling balefully into the cracks in the concrete. I am more circumspect next plunge and muse that a direct hit would have been most embarrassing, involving sidling back to our table with hands crossed virginally in front of my trousers. However, I emerge unscathed by soap or bugs, clothing intact. Altogether a minor triumph given L's rather low opinion of my ability to feed or generally behave in public without requiring a launderette afterwards.

ooooooooOoooooooo

A couple of weeks later, I am lying awake at 3am listening to L who has been unwittingly impregnated by some hideous foreign virus. She is heavy with cold, blissfully fast asleep and snarling like a cornered tiger; meanwhile a circus-ring full of elephants plays hop-scotch on the ceiling. The noise is ear ringing; talk about an orchestra tuning up. I decide that a small pack of young nocturnal lizards must have entered the loft cavity through a ventilation grill, prospered and got stuck in there. The trick is to persuade the beggars to vacate—midnight tea dances by large mammals are not an option. In time though I am able to get back to sleep—our palm trees outside are now big enough so that their fronds rustling gently in the breeze sound like light rain and have a wonderfully soporific effect.

One of the pleasures of the night in The Bahamas occurs when there is about to be, or has been, a recent downpour and the frogs come out to play. Battalions of them emerge from Heaven knows where, totally crazed and shamelessly sex-starved, desperately selling themselves with brazen abandon: Bahamian frogs don't "rivet" they very definitely "quaack". The noise is a deafening thunderous roll of sound, like an orchestra of hyperventilating ducks tuning up—this is no demure courtship! One particular beast irritates L by yelling, "I don't care, I don't care, I don't care," just outside the bedroom window. I am sympathetic to her plight within reason but have never heard this phenomenon, being deaf to its precise frequency and thus, am open to accusation for, firstly sleeping like a hog and, secondly lacking the imagination to translate frog-song accurately.

ooooooooOoooooooo

We have a three legged washing machine—one leg having rusted away in the salt, sea atmosphere. This is fine when it is merely at rest as an "objet d'art" so to speak and a partial solution to this problem is achieved by placing a prosthetic wooden chock underneath the washer where the leg would be. The machine is not big and it squats innocuously in the utility room unremarked except when called upon to perform, about three times weekly. On these occasions however as the saying goes it "punches well above its weight". My dear wife, like most people I suppose, has moments of mind-boggling profligacy followed by spells of remorseless parsimony that would warm Scrooge's heart. But she is unsurpassed, even by a pharaoh's slave master when loading the washer. Every cubic millimetre is called into action as a wondrous collection of hairy beach towels, tennis kit, pairs of languid trousers, stiff swimming trunks and wardrobes of under clothes are stuffed into its maw with vigour: lastly, the door is jammed closed in Japanese metro style, any slow-moving garments being reprimanded by a good hard shove. "Start" is pressed and the machine is left to do what automatics do. When it has ingested enough water to make a paste of the contents the motor valiantly commences the spin. It is a testament to the robustness of the machine that it tries to work at all with the additional deadweight. However, it does and such is the cacophony it could shout "Vive l'empereur!" and one could believe that the Old Guard was marching up the hill at Waterloo. This is matched by a thumping as of many boots as the machine reaches warp drive crossing the utility room floor making for the door like a Dalek on steroids. Order is restored by throwing our bodies selflessly in its path to jab the power button before being mown down. After due (and repetitious) exclamations of surprise the load is halved and the process repeated without further incident.

But all is not lost for this revelation results in a trip to the Corner Launderette which is resolutely not on any corner but is easily recognisable because steam issues from a ventilatory crack in the masonry and it has an iconic 'signature' derelict washing machine loitering outside in an insouciant manner. Definitely a Brave New World.

oooooooooOooooooooo

However, not content with having found the launderette my wife has determined to exact revenge on the washer for its aberrant behaviour and has crept up on it unawares, thrown miscellaneous indigestible items into its mouth and punched "start". The poor machine protests loudly, sounding as though it is getting a good kicking. As it turns out, this is hardly surprising for, as we rush to its assistance I bellow, "What's in it?" "Oh, I'm just washing some pairs of shoes," L responds airily.

CHAPTER 40

By request, I am on the jetty waiting to board our friend Howard's immaculate brilliant white 21ft Twin Vee as it lies, gently bobbing in the calm water of Victoria Pond. He has invited me and mutual friend Don to go fishing. Although I am not greatly enthusiastic about this sport (I find that sea swell, and the unique perfume of diesel exhaust fumes and gently sun-rotting bait combined with trying to handle a dipping fishing rod with a line and hook like a swaying cobra are a pretty toxic combination) I feel an obligation to answer the call of social duty. His fine boat is a twin-hulled, stable, sea-going platform with a "bimini" canvas shade stretched over the top a bit like the "Surrey with the fringe" and two shiny black Suzuki 150 horsepower outboard motors. The sea and the sky are nearly matched in the same glassy pale blue with only the slightest breeze to ruffle the water here and there. All in all it is a beautiful morning. A certain amount of rugged badinage is exchanged in the best tradition of American "buddy" activities: a necessary precursor to any sporting event such as we are embarking on, so it seems. Rods, bait and the essential beers (another area fraught with danger for those of a fragile disposition) are loaded aboard and off we go.

At this point it is important to declare my credentials. I am no expert on fishing but occasionally drive the boat for Quentin, a good friend who specialises in catching Barracuda. This is not because I am good at it or because I find it mesmerically enjoyable but driving keeps one's brain occupied, one's eyes on the horizon and avoids having to deal with rods, bait etc and inevitably revisiting one's breakfast at an inopportune moment. As far as I can see, fishing is as war or, indeed, cricket has been described, immense periods of stultifying boredom interspersed with moments of frenetic, chaotic and often pointless activity. Quentin employs serious hardware to subdue the Barracuda. Firstly a pair of mailed gloves which he wears when handling the brutes, no minnows at up to 6ft : secondly, a pair of long surgical forceps with which to extract his hook, avoiding the razor sharp teeth: thirdly, a hefty and piratical looking steel gaff which he hooks into their jaws to haul them out of the ocean from beside the boat without presenting an inadvertent snack of human limb and then, after removing the hook, he wallops them over the head several times before dropping them into the "live bait" locker. His boat is a Boston Whaler "Dauntless" which dips and bucks on the ocean swell as he baits lines, catches and stows the fish in an impressively businesslike manner. I drive and watch.

As Howard's Twin Vee glides under the bridge to the ocean we receive a laconic wave from three Bahamians sitting idly on the harbour wall. Once out in the open sea the two "Good Old Boys" set up and bait their rods. Having no rod of my own I offer to drive but this is declined—Howard exerts a proprietary nervousness over his favourite toy which, because he is the island's vet is called, not unreasonably "Vet's Pet".

Some considerable time passes without any bites and initial enthusiasm begins to fade together with visions of freezers laden with fresh fish. As the conversation becomes less bullish and more intermittent I venture to ask what the procedure might be if we were actually to catch something. Looks of surprise cross both faces,

"What do you mean? . . . . we'll just pull them in!"

"Steady chaps" I say, "Lets just hypothesise it's a 4ft barracuda for the sake of argument."

"Er . . . . well that's down to you."

"OK, so where are the gloves?"

"What gloves?"

"To grip it with." Silence. "Oh, . . . and what will I use to take the hook out?"

"You hold it and someone will pull."

"Where's your gaff?"

"What gaff, what for?"

"To haul the fish out of the water."

". . . . Oh."

"And how do I subdue it . . . . have you got a hammer?" Hoots of laughter.

"Hell no!"

"Well in that case, given the standard of our equipment I hope to God we don't catch anything!"

We didn't, returning empty-handed after another hour. I haven't been invited again. We remain great friends, but . . . .

oooooooo0ooooooooo

The outside 'pool bar' at the Peace and Plenty would not be the same without Lerman the evergreen barman. Allegedly, the inventor of the "Goombay Smash" cocktail, Lerman is often known as 'Doc' since some wag procured a pseudo diploma awarding him a 'Doctorate of libation' for his efforts. His enthusiasm (although he can get distinctly testy, not to say downright truculent, during Regatta) has more recently earned him the accolade of "Employee of the Year" and he is an enthusiastic supporter of the "Bahamian brush-up," that is, topping up one's drinks. I unwisely told him that I am writing this so now, every time I see him he booms across the bar, "You gotta put me in your book, man! . . . . Gotta be in your book!" And so here he is.

oooooooo0ooooooo

The contents of the shelves in Exuma Markets, one of the George Town supermarkets reveals one of its pearls today. I am rooting around the chemicals looking for some cheap shampoo when, like Alice in Wonderland, I come across a single plastic jar on the homeopathic shelf marked "Horny Goat Weed." Curiosity aroused, I deliberate as to whether the weed might look in its natural state like a goat's horns or, less likely, whether it is an extract from a randy goat. Is this Exuma's answer to Rhino horn? I pick up the jar and reverse it to read more, half expecting it to say "Drink me!" It actually says "Horny Goat Weed with Maca (whatever that is) are herbs celebrated around the world and are prized for their ability to conjure up the passionate nature in men to provide you and your mate with a memorable night of romance." There is no advice as to whether it should be administered internally or externally (the French and Spanish can get quite memorably excited about using suppositories, after all) and I consider how starved of experience must my love life have been never to have come across such an essential aid. Resisting the temptation to make an impulse purchase I return home gleefully and regale L with the details of my unique find, pointing out that there is to be a forthcoming wedding of two middle-aged friends of ours on the island. She laughs nervously. "It would make a really good wedding present for the couple with nearly everything," I enthuse. L thinks not. In truth, the groom is a bit older than the bride and has an enormous sexual ego of dubious provenance. Ah well, another good idea on the cutting room floor.

CHAPTER 41

I am not good at crises which occur when I am asleep and the other night was a good example. I am in what the experts call deep sleep at 3 am when L suddenly hisses at me in a searing stage whisper, "Are you AWAKE?" No danger of sleeping through this—it is as though a jet aircraft has just buzzed my right ear.

"Uh . . . yes," I respond automatically.

"What's that noise?"

Consciousness is slowly returning and instinctively I grab the alarm clock and wrestle with it.

"What the hell's the matter with this thing—I can't turn it off."

"It's the PHONE you BF!"

"What, where?" I cry plaintively and catapult out of bed to grab the extension land-line from the dressing table in a repeat wrestle of the alarm clock.

"It's the Vonage phone in the SPARE ROOM for goodness sake."

"Oh . . . , ah." I run to the door and sprint across the darkened sitting room and into the spare room just it time to lift the receiver before cut-off. "Hello" I whisper hoarsely into the mouthpiece. A vibrantly perky voice replies on the other end "OH HELLO! . ." and asks to speak to L. However, I have been scrupulously drilled in the gatekeeper role and even at this dire hour swing into that well practised routine like the seasoned professional I am.

"Er, who is speaking, please?" I mutter weakly.

"Oh it's SAMANTHA from Marks and Spencer's, Baker Street."

"Um, ... you probably don't realise it but you are . . , er, actually talking to me in the Bahamas and it's 3 am in the middle of the . . , um, night." With a hint of desperation. And then, inspirationally, "I wonder if she could ring you back, say, in the morning . . . . it might be a little more convenient?"

"OH, I'M TERRIBLY SORRY!" yells the chirpy Samantha. I take her details and promise to pass them on. I stumble back to our bedroom and slide inconspicuously, so I think, back under the sheet.

"What on earth was that all about?"

I murmur, "Oh nothing dear, just Marks and Spencer's . . . ." Zzzzzzzzzzz.

ooooooooOooooooo

Underneath the house, below the filter on the "city water" mains supply a hole is appearing in the ground. To begin with I am in denial and convince myself that it has always existed or is merely the result of a collapse into some small underground cavity that was always there. Job done, it is buried in my subconscious below more pressing matters such as whether to spray the lime tree with pesticide. Some days later L fixes me with a penetrating look.

"There's something you ought to see," she says.

"What sort of something?"

"You ought to see it—it's under the house."

"Really?" I respond innocently, nerves jangling in case this is the prelude to a complex and expensive disaster.

"Is it a hole, by any chance?" I enquire optimistically.

"Yes, have you seen it? I think we have got a <u>serious</u> rat problem."

"Surely not, I haven't seen any—is the hole by the water filter?"

"Oh, so you've seen it?"

"I'm not sure, show me where your hole is and I'll see if it's the same as mine."

We trundle down under. Sure enough it is "our" hole, much enlarged with a significant heap of spoil beside it. After frightening ourselves with guesses of how many rats it would take to construct the entrance to such a drift mine a small shaft of reality peeks in. We alert ourselves to the attractive possibility that it might be a land crab.

"I tell you what," I say with conviction, "They are nocturnal so when I put the rubbish out last thing I'll sneak down to the filter with a torch and leap out turning it on at the last minute."

"All right," says L with muted relief.

The problem has now been relegated to her subconscious.

The hour grows late so I arm myself with the torch and steal down stairs. Fingers crossed I leap round the corner and flash it on. And there he is, a splendid great big old land crab stark white in the torchlight sitting at the edge of the hole—he must be at least nine inches across his shell alone. For a second he is transfixed by the beam and then he scuttles down into his home. I dowse the torch and retreat swiftly out of courtesy. Back upstairs I am interrogated.

"You were right," I allow, "It was an enormous rat!—no really, it was a superb land crab."

We tiptoe back down so that L can see but he has not reappeared. One performance a night is quite enough.

The next day I carefully lay fresh earth at the entrance to the hole in an endeavour to find out where he goes. But the earth remains undisturbed—sadly my invasive activity of the previous evening must have been enough to encourage him to move on.

ooooooooOooooooooo

As we sit doing the tourist thing in the early evening sunshine on the water's edge dandling our feel in the sea at Chat 'n' Chill drinking Goombay Smashes L admires the plastic chairs which are the source of our comfort. They are of a particular design, originally made with flat planks of wood, called Adirondacks. I pay them little heed—apart from the fact that they appear to come in a range of colours, one plastic chair is much like another, generally hard on the backside without a cushion. Unbeknown to me, L's acquisitive processes are being stimulated and swinging into action. That evening discovering that friends of ours Andy and Debbie are going up to Nassau to get a pallet of 'this and that' shipped down, she slips them a small order of her own.

Some days later there is a tinkle of the hand-bell that is our doorbell (it can be irritating when it's windy) and Andy and Debbie are revealed, with their truck. L's incipient kleptomania has been at work and on the back of the truck is not one but two pairs of Adirondacks basking iridescently in the sunlight. "Hope you like the colour," enthuses Andy peering at our faces, "You did say you wanted them to be bright." Slightly less enthusiastic, a hint of uncertainty creeping in. "You can have the other ones if you want, we don't mind". As we know that whichever ones we don't have they will keep, this latter offer is not a serious option and, in any event, the other ones are the strikingly novel colour of a child's sandpit on a wet day; pale vomit-green. Bright is a masterly understatement for ours; these chairs presumably named after the Adirondack mountains for reasons which become apparent when one sits in them are called "Dolomiti fucsia" (so the Italians have a hand in it somewhere) and are, as the name implies, a hideously lurid shade of bilious pink. L accepts them with gushing enthusiasm: I am nonplussed and as a defence tactic maintain an inscrutably poker face sufficient I hope to hide my sense of artistic outrage. After our friends have left with the happy smiles of those with a job well done she turns, "Heavens what are we going to do with those!? What a lurid colour." "Perhaps we'll put them under the house until we decide what to do with them," I venture. This is agreed and there they languish while L pursues various stratagems to dispose of them including swapping them for other goods and beguiling Marco, the local garden centre owner, to take possession and sell them. (He knows a market leader when he sees one and declines this unique and never to be repeated offer—he's no fool).

Eventually, they are reinstated: after all, "They do provide additional seating options for us when it's windy," and put well out of sight at the furthest end of our south verandah, thereby minimising this social gaffe.

Some days later I come across L resplendent in Irish emerald green gaucho pants and matching tee shirt curled up on one of them. "You look just like a frog on a lily pad," I say, cheerfully. She raises an eyebrow, "Thank you for that gratuitous compliment." And with that the subject slams closed like the trapdoor of doom.

Beware the Adirondack

We are spending the evening with Simon and Cynthia. During the course of supper I tell an anecdote which amuses the company.

"That's another one for the diary," laughs Cynthia.

"You're right!" I agree. The following morning at breakfast I recall the incident but not the tale.

"What was that story I told last night?" I ask.

"I don't know, what was it?" L replies distractedly.

Why is it that I can never remember the better stories the next day?

End

POSTSCRIPT

The anecdotes in this book have covered a period of several years and whilst they are not in strict sequence I have tried to give them an approximate seasonal chronology. Inevitably, life on Exuma is not a snapshot but a continuum and since this has been published a number of aspects have changed:

We learnt recently of the sad death of Howard de Young, the island's vet—a great loss of a good friend to us and an irreplaceable expertise to the island—he will be a very big miss.

The four Seasons hotel has gone from the north end of the island, replaced by Sandals, an "all in" resort operation, whose business philosophy has resulted in a number of extra air flights including a direct service from Toronto to George Town. Exuma needs its tourists.

The Peace and Plenty has leased its Hamburger Bay beach bar to Big D who is making a decent job of selling fast, economic lunches and evening events while still running "Big D's Conch Spot" up island.

Sam's site in George Town including Sam's Place, the offices and shops underneath, the filling station and the docks has been sold

entire to "fast" Eddie Irvine the former formula 1 racing driver. What his Irish blarney (for he's got it in spades) will achieve remains to be seen! But he has ambitious plans.

The Peace and plenty Bonefish Lodge is under new ownership and substantial renovations are taking place.

Exuma markets now receives a container of goodies direct from the States each week and their beef is unsurpassed. Most delicacies one can think of can be ordered if they are not in stock.

Our friends Peter and Trish left Exuma last year "for good—done that," but couldn't stay away and have bought a new car and boat to celebrate their return.

But, all in all, the island is still as sleepy, sunny and close to paradise. We long to return when we are away—it simply gets into the blood and the call is as strong as ever.